THE VISIGOTHS
IN THE TIME OF ULFILA

T0353231

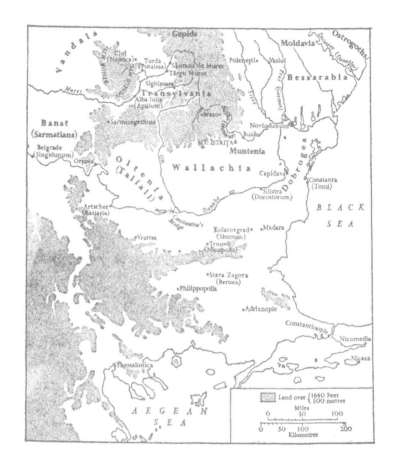

Gothia in the Fourth Century

THE VISIGOTHS
IN THE TIME
OF ULFILA

Second Edition

E.A. Thompson

Foreword by Michael Kulikowski

Duckworth

Second edition 2008
Gerald Duckworth & Co. Ltd.
90-93 Cowcross Street, London EC1M 6BF
Tel: 020 7490 7300
Fax: 020 7490 0080
info@duckworth-publishers.co.uk
www.ducknet.co.uk

First edition published in 1966 by Oxford University Press
Reprinted by permission.

Foreword © 2008 by Michael Kulikowski

Appendix 4 © 1991 by John Matthews
Reprinted by permission of Liverpool University Press

All rights reserved. No part of this publication
may be reproduced, stored in a retrieval system, or
transmitted, in any form or by any means, electronic,
mechanical, photocopying, recording or otherwise,
without the prior permission of the publisher.

A catalogue record for this book is available
from the British Library

ISBN 978 0 7156 3700 5

FOREWORD TO THE SECOND EDITION

Michael Kulikowski, University of Tennessee

E.A. Thompson published his *Visigoths in the Time of Ulfila* in 1966. It served to sum up his researches into early Gothic history at a time when he was working on the monumental, monographic *Goths in Spain* (Oxford, 1969). By contrast with that later work, the small volume that appeared in 1966 was composed of quite thoroughly rewritten versions of previously published work. As Thompson states in his own preface, four of six chapters originally appeared as articles elsewhere. And yet, unlike so many volumes of collected essays (and indeed unlike Thompson's own later collection, *Romans and Barbarians*), *The Visigoths in the Time of Ulfila* is much more than the cobbling together of *disiecta membra*. It offers a full and coherent vision of Gothic history before the Danube crossing of 376, and it is because of that coherent vision that the book retains its very substantial value to the present day. Much work has been done on Gothic history since Thompson wrote, and many books – probably far too many – have been published on the subject. That is perhaps unavoidable: Gothic history is inextricable from the problem of Rome's fall, an inexhaustible topic, whether for ancient historians, medievalists or the public at large. Every scholarly generation offers us several new versions of the Goths, emphases shifting slightly within a relatively stable narrative. In so crowded a field, something rather more than shifting emphasis is needed to give a work the permanence enjoyed by *The Visigoths in the Time of Ulfila*.

The book's permanence, one might suggest, lies in the fact that – although it is, of course, a work of its time – its fundamental insights were well ahead of that time. Perhaps most significantly, Thompson was willing to take barbarian, non-Roman society seriously, not as a timeless, prehistoric *Germanentum*, but as a social world fit for just as complex an analysis as the world of the Greeks and Romans, if only one could tease that analysis out of sparse and clouded sources. This was – and, sadly, can still be – a rare approach in a scholar trained as an ancient historian, for it is all too easy to adopt the terms of analysis used in our sources, all of them Graeco-Roman, and thus to define barbarians in Roman terms, as wild, dangerous and more or less indistinguishable one from the other. Simply because he succeeded in examining the fourth-century Goths in their own right, Thompson's work remains current, despite some obvious signs of age: Thompson is, for instance, very ready to look for comparative evidence for the Goths among other 'Germanic' peoples (that is, any people who spoke a Germanic language), however far removed in time or place they might be. For all that, however, Thompson is constantly aware of change, of the power of time and historical circumstance to alter cultural behaviours.

This awareness of, and sensitivity to, cultural change stems from the cultural materialism – the Marxism to which he had converted by 1939 – that lies at the heart of Thompson's interpretations. Old-school British social history hardly exists any longer as an analytical mode. It is therefore increasingly difficult nowadays to recognize Thompson's innovation: he took an analytical framework native to the modern, indeed the industrial, age and applied it to the history of the later Roman empire, taking seriously the notion that the means of production, the distribution and control of wealth, was a primary motive force in ancient society, even ancient society beyond the Roman frontier. Before Thompson, class could be discussed in Roman terms, labour perhaps less so, but neither in any meaningful sense outside the empire. The fundamental insight of Thompson's cultural materialism – that 'private property meant social power, and the poor man was a political cipher' (p. 72) – lends continued power to his analysis of Gothic society, an analysis that he himself drew from written sources alone, but that we can now document on the basis of ever-increasing archaeological evidence. More and more scholars are returning, by way of post-colonial anthropology and sociology, to a perspective Thompson derived from his instinctive understanding of how societies work when material resources are unequal. Empires change their less sophisticated neighbours merely by existing. They work upon neighbouring polities even when they do not consciously try to do so, though of course they often do try, and their actions generally serve to break down existing social unities and reconstitute them in a more hierarchical fashion. Thompson, for his part, addressed this phenomenon most explicitly when he considered the breakdown of Visigothic tribal religion; if we are nowadays less sure of what 'Visigothic tribal religion' might actually mean, Thompson's analysis of why the breakdown he detected took place was fundamentally sound. Roman influence on neighbouring tribes and states was inescapable, and it inescapably broke down old certainties, reconstituted them into new, and newly hierarchical, shapes: wealth, armour, better weapons and better-organized armies where before there had been the social parity that poverty enforces. It requires commitment to neither cultural materialism nor postcolonial theory to see how widely applicable this insight is along Roman frontiers, and not just among the Goths of the fourth century.

There have been two major interpretative trends in Gothic studies since Thompson wrote. The first is associated with the concept of ethnogenesis, now widely used by early medievalists to describe the coming into being of barbarian ethnic groups. Ethnogenesis is most closely associated with the Viennese historian Herwig Wolfram, whose history of the Goths remains the seminal work in this school. To generalize broadly, ethnogenesis-theory presumes that ethnicity is the central component of barbarian identity, and thus that ethnicity is the central fact of barbarian history. It goes on to argue, however, that barbarian ethnicity was not a matter of genuine descent-communities. On the contrary, ethnicity was the province of *Traditionskerne* ('nuclei of tradition' in English), small groups of aristocratic warriors who carried ethnic traditions with them from place to place and transmitted ethnic identity from generation to generation; larger ethnic groups coalesced and dissolved around these nuclei of tradition in a process of continuous ethnic reinvention – ethnogenesis. There was, in other words, no stable Gothic tribe, no large number of ethnic Goths, but rather Gothic ethnic traditions, carried by Gothic noble families and adopted by the heterogeneous individuals who chose to join them. Despite certain problems in its application – most especially a reliance on the narrative of the sixth-century Constantinopolitan writer Jordanes as an authentic transmitter of Gothic ethnic traditions – ethnogenesis-theory has been very influential among medieval historians working on the barbarians.

For classicists and ancient historians, by contrast, two

different approaches have tended to dominate, one a revival of interpretations popular more than a century ago, the other in some ways rather close to the vision of E.A. Thompson himself. In British scholarship, a much older vision of the barbarians, particularly the Goths, has come forcefully back into vogue. In this approach, barbarian identity and barbarian ethnicity are not problematic at all. Tribal homelands existed, back in the forests of Germany. Migration was a real, large-scale phenomenon, and ethnic consciousness, if not necessarily political identity, stayed the same even when tribes packed up and hit the road. Although this approach has the virtue of simplicity, it shares similar interpretative limitations with ethnogenesis, since both retain narratives of distant migration in one guise or other, and both privilege the perspective of hindsight: looking at the barbarians not in the light of contemporary sources as members of a Roman imperial commonwealth, but as outsiders whose destiny it was to destroy and replace Rome. Thompson, though he believed in both real barbarian tribes and in migration, never made that mistake. For him, barbarian history, and particularly the Gothic history that he treated as paradigmatic, had always to be seen according to the circumstances of its own time and place, not within a larger, teleological narrative. A final interpretative trend visible in recent work by ancient historians develops upon the perspective of Thompson himself: developments along the Roman frontier are seen as a product of the Roman empire, social artefacts created by Roman interference in the life of neighbouring societies, both directly and by way of example, so that, for instance, the rise of powerful Gothic leadership in the 350s and 360s is in part a consequence of deliberate Roman policy in the aftermath of Constantine's victories of the 330s.

The foregoing approaches are matters of interpretation – their varying emphases do not depend to any great extent on different views of historical events. There has, in fact, been only one truly decisive change in scholarly interpretations of the Goths since Thompson wrote, and that is in our ability to identify a group of barbarians called Visigoths in the fourth century. Contemporary fourth-century sources do not speak of Visigoths and Ostrogoths – they speak of Tervingi and Greuthungi. When Thompson wrote, scholars assumed as he did that the Tervingi were the Visigoths and the Greuthungi the Ostrogoths before each group crossed the Danube. Nowadays, and regardless of theoretical predilections, there is a general consensus that no simple correspondence between Tervingian and Visigoth exists. On the contrary, the Danube crossing was a catastrophic moment that created a brand new group of Goths, the group that settled in the Balkans. Some part of this group – how large a part is disputed – then followed Alaric west, and ultimately created a kingdom in Gaul under his successors. The Tervingian name disappeared because the political identity that sustained it had disappeared. For ethnogenesis-scholars that is a function of the weakness and small scale of any barbarian ethnic identity – all that mattered were the bearers of Gothic ethnic traditions, who reconstituted a new Visigothic identity on Roman soil. For proponents of large scale migration – and also for those who see fourth-century Gothic developments as a fundamentally provincial and Roman phenomenon – it is because the Goths who settled in the Balkans in 382, those who followed Alaric, and even more so the Goths who left Italy with Athaulf, were a very heterogeneous set of Gothic groups, not just Tervingi. In either reading, however, the title of Thompson's book becomes its only major defect: there were no 'Visigoths' in the time of Ulfila.

Our understanding of most of the material in Thompson's book has not changed radically, and controversy still surrounds the correct date of Ulfila's consecration and that of the wider Gothic conversion to Christianity. Archaeology is now far more advanced than it was when Thompson was writing, but he made little use of archaeology in any of his many works. Perhaps most importantly, where forty years ago we knew very little about anything save the sorts of objects placed in graves, we now know a great deal about unspectacular domestic and rural environments throughout non-Roman Europe. The material remains of the Sântana-de-Mures/Cernjachov archaeological culture, which extended across the whole region in which fourth-century Goths dwelt, now give us a fairly nuanced picture of a settled agricultural society, made up of exactly the sort of small village which Thompson described on the basis of the literary evidence of the *Passio Sabae* (a translation of which is included in the present volume as Appendix 4). It is a sign of Thompson's fine historical instinct that he could recognize the intrinsic value of the *Passio* for social history, and that we can now see that evidence strikingly confirmed by settlement archaeology. *The Visigoths in the Time of Ulfila* remains one of the best books ever written on the history of any barbarian group of the Roman era. The present edition will allow a new generation of readers to discover as much for themselves.

Bibliographical Note

A great deal has been written about the Goths in the past forty years and a comprehensive bibliography would be very long indeed. Thompson's own further writings on the subject were collected in *Romans and Barbarians: The Decline of the Western Empire* (Madison, WI, 1982), while his earlier, and highly relevant, book on the Huns was reissued with a new afterword as *The Huns* (Oxford, 1996). Much the most important recent contribution to the literature has been Peter Heather, *Goths and Romans, 332-489* (Oxford, 1991), which established chronology and the limits of the evidence on a sounder footing than had ever previously been achieved. Heather has also written a highly traditional survey of Gothic history, *The Goths* (Oxford, 1996). There is an awful lot of ethnogenesis literature on the market, Herwig Wolfram's *History of the Goths* (1979; English trans., Berkeley, 1988) the most widely available and influential. My own views on the whole subject are published in *Rome's Gothic Wars from the Third Century to Alaric* (Cambridge, 2007). For new approaches to the barbarians more generally, two important works are Hugh Elton's *Warfare in Roman Europe* (Oxford, 1996), which contains much good sense about barbarian society and how warfare worked in it, and John Drinkwater, *The Alamanni and Rome, 213-496* (Oxford, 2007), a work with which one suspects Thompson would have sympathized.

On specific points, N. Lenski, 'The Gothic Civil War and the Date of the Gothic Conversion', *Greek, Roman and Byzantine Studies* 36 (1995), 51-87, is a study of a topic that Thompson may have dismissed too rapidly, while on Valens more generally, we have the same author's *Failure of Empire* (Berkeley, 2004). The state of the evidence for the Sântana-de-Mures/Cernjachov as it stood in the 1980s is summarized in Peter Heather and John Matthews, *The Goths in the Fourth Century* (Liverpool, 1991), which also includes the translation of the *Passio Sabae* reprinted at the end of the present volume; Michel Kazanski's *Les Goths* (Paris, 1989), is well-illustrated, but very old fashioned in its approach; the same and more could be said of Pere de Palol and Gisela Ripoll, *Die Goten: Geschichte und Kunst in Westeuropa* (Stuttgart, 1990). More theoretically informed is the indispensable study of Guy Halsall, *Barbarian Migrations and the Roman West 376-568* (Cambridge, 2007), which embodies ideas about history, archaeology and social change which he developed at greater length in specialist studies over the years.

Only two editions of importance to *The Visigoths in the Time of Ulfila* have appeared since Thompson wrote. Auxentius has been published in a new edition, *Epistula de fide, uita et obitu Vlfilae*, ed. R. Gryson (Turnhout, 1978; translated in Heather and Matthews [1989]); while the two-volume Teubner edition of Ammianus Marcellinus by. W. Seyfarth (1978) improves dramatically on the text of Rolfe from which Thompson worked.

PREFACE

THE Visigoths are the only fourth-century invaders of the Roman Empire of whom we have detailed information. The Alamanni, the Vandals, the Ostrogoths, and the others are mentioned frequently enough by Roman writers, but for the most part only in general terms: they were remote from the great centres of power and of literary production, and indeed during the whole of the fourth century they remained outside the Imperial frontiers. Hence our knowledge of their material development and their social organization in the days of Constantine and Theodosius can hardly be said to exist. But throughout the first three quarters of the fourth century the Visigoths were living in the former Roman province of Dacia, immediately north of the lower Danube, in what is now approximately Rumania, and so were all but on the doorstep of Constantinople. Their traders and warriors were not unfamiliar sights south of the great river, and Roman influence upon them was more extensive than upon any other Germanic people at this date. Moreover, when the Huns drove them south of the Danube in 376, they became the first major barbarian people to be accepted into the Empire *en bloc* and to be provided with land there by the Imperial authorities. And finally, when they began to move westwards in 395, their journey took them to the main centres of Roman civilization in Europe: apart from Constantinople, they penetrated into Greece, into Italy (where they captured Rome itself in 410), into southern France, and finally into Spain, so that Roman writers were obliged willy nilly to speak of them in some detail.

Thanks to the labours of Ulfila (to give him the Latin form of his name, or Wulfilas, as philologists sometimes call him, or Urphilas, as his name appears in some Greek writers), Gothic literature is older by some centuries than the literature of any other Germanic people, even though little of it has survived apart from the fragments of the Gothic Bible. Again, largely owing to the preliminary work of Ulfila, the Visigoths were the first Germanic people to be converted to Christianity; and we must begin with them if we are to study the earliest history of Christianity among the Germans.

The student of Roman history, then, or of Germanic languages, or of the expansion of the Christian Church may find some value in a study of the society which produced Ulfila, the apostle of the Goths and the father of Germanic literature. I shall have little to say about the theological conflicts in which Ulfila became involved and nothing at all about the technicalities of the Gothic language: my concern is solely with Visigothic society. It must be emphasized at the very beginning, however, that, although we know more about the Visigoths than about any other fourth-century Germanic people, yet our constant handicap will be shortage of evidence. To most of the major questions we can at best give dim and shadowy answers; and to some of them—for example, why did the Visigoths accept Arian rather than Catholic Christianity?—we can give no answer at all.

What were the Visigoths like, then, during the lifetime of their greatest man? This book begins with an outline of their political history to the year 395. I do not give any detailed account of their invasions of the Roman Empire: all these will be found set out in English in the first volume of the *Cambridge Medieval*

History. I then turn to their material culture, their social organization, and (a subject of which we know very little) their paganism in the days of Ulfila. I deal next with a Greek document of the highest value, the *Passion of St. Saba,* which introduces us not only to village life among the Visigoths (a subject which none of our other authorities touches upon) but also to the conditions in which the early Visigothic Christians lived and in some cases died for their faith. The problem then confronts us of the date at which the bulk of the Visigoths were converted to Christianity, and discussion of this question entails looking at the first Christian missionaries who went across the lower Danube. Thereafter the evidence, such as it is, for the earliest history of Visigothic Christianity after the general conversion is assembled and discussed, though the discussion here is even more inconclusive than elsewhere in the book owing to the lack of evidence: we can do little more than formulate some of the problems. I end with a consideration of some matters which occurred after Ulfila was dead and which throw light on Visigothic Christianity at the end of the fourth century and the beginning of the fifth.

Chapters Two, Three, Four, and Five appeared originally in *Nottingham Medieval Studies, Historia,* the *Journal of Ecclesiastical History,* and *Latomus* respectively. I have largely re-cast them, and publish them here with the permission of the editors of those journals. Appendix Three contains the substance of a paper which originally appeared in German in the *Zeitschrift für deutsches Altertum*: this, too, is printed with the editor's permission.

I am grateful to my friend Dr. R. H. Osborne, of the University of Nottingham, for help in drawing up the map.

CONTENTS

CONTENTS

ABBREVIATIONS

Amm. Marc.: Ammianus Marcellinus, ed. C. U. Clark (Berlin, 1910–15). Ammianus is the chief source for the political and military history of the years 353–78.

Auxentius: The edition of the text of Auxentius' letter on Ulfila cited by page and line of F. Kauffmann, *Aus der Schule des Wulfila*, Texte und Untersuchungen zur altgermanischen Religionsgeschichte, i (Strasbourg, 1899). But note the criticisms of this edition by F. Vogt, *Anzeiger für deutsches Altertum und deutsche Litteratur*, xxviii (1902), 190–213.

Beiträge: *Beiträge zur Geschichte der deutschen Sprache und Literatur*.

Chron. Min.: T. Mommsen, *Chronica Minora*, 3 vols. After citations of the Chronicles I add in brackets a reference to the volume and page of Mommsen.

CIL: *Corpus Inscriptionum Latinarum*.

Delehaye: H. Delehaye, 'Saints de Thrace et de Mésie', *Analecta Bollandiana*, xxxi (1912), 161–300, who gives the Greek text of the *Passion of St. Saba* at 216–21, and also the texts of the Gothic Calendar, the *Passio SS. Innae, Rimae, et Pinae*, and the *Passio S. Nicetae*.

Dessau, *ILS*: H. Dessau, *Inscriptiones Latinae Selectae*.

Fiebiger: O. Fiebiger, *Inschriftensammlung zur Geschichte der Ostgermanen*, Neue Folge, Denkschriften d. Akademie der Wissenschaften in Wien: phil.-hist. Klasse, Bd. 70, Abh. 3 (Vienna and Leipzig, 1939).

JHS: *Journal of Hellenic Studies*.

JTS: *Journal of Theological Studies*.

Neues Archiv: *Neues Archiv der Gesellschaft für ältere deutsche Geschichtskunde.*

Passion or *Passio*: See Delehaye above.

P.-W.: Pauly-Wissowa, *Realencyclopädie.*

RB: *Revue bénédictine.*

Seeck, *Untergang*: Otto Seeck, *Geschichte des Untergangs der antiken Welt*, 6 vols.

SHA: Scriptores Historiae Augustae, ed. D. Magie (Loeb Library), 3 vols.

Thompson, *EG*: E. A. Thompson, *The Early Germans* (Oxford, 1965).

ZfdA: *Zeitschrift für deutsches Altertum.*

INTRODUCTION

ULFILA is mentioned a few times by the fifth-century Greek ecclesiastical historians Socrates, Sozomen, and Theodoret, who were orthodox Catholics, and Philostorgius, who was not: he was a Eunomian heretic, and so his work has survived only in a paraphrase. Ulfila is also mentioned by the sixth-century historian Jordanes, who, as a Goth, might have been expected to say more of him than in fact he does: one solitary sentence is all that he gives to the great Gothic bishop. But the most valuable document relating to him was written in the fourth century immediately after he died. This is the surviving part of a letter of Auxentius, bishop of Durostorum (near Silistra in Bulgaria), who was a pupil of his. In this letter, which was not discovered until 1840, the author speaks of the life of Ulfila, whom he knew well, and discusses and quotes the creed which he wrote at the very end of his life.[1]

Ulfila was born about the year 311, presumably somewhere in Rumania. On one side of his family he was descended from Roman prisoners who had been carried off from Asia Minor by a raiding band of Goths shortly after the middle of the third century. The barbarians had captured them at their village of Sadagolthina near the town of Parnassus in the Roman

[1] The sources for Ulfila's life are conveniently printed in W. Streitberg, *Die gotische Bibel* (Heidelberg, 1908), xiii ff. For an old but useful assessment of them see G. Kaufmann, 'Kritische Untersuchung der Quellen zur Geschichte Ulfilas', *ZfdA*, xxvii (1883), 193–261. For a brief introduction to the life of Ulfila with select literature see A. Lippold, P.-W., ix A. i. 512–31.

province of Cappadocia.[1] The prisoners from Asia Minor taken in this and other raids were in many cases Christians, who did not abandon their beliefs when calamity overtook them; and no doubt Ulfila was brought up as a Christian in a predominantly pagan society. Nothing is known of his education; but he had reached the office of 'reader' (*lector*) in the Church in Gothia by the time he was thirty years of age. It was an office which entailed some study of the Bible and was a good preparation for his future career as a translator. The Gothic church services were conducted in the Gothic language,[2] so that Ulfila even at this date may have had to translate as well as to read.

Philostorgius tells us that in the reign of Constantine, in circumstances of which we know nothing, the Visigoths sent Ulfila and some others as ambassadors to the Roman Empire, and there he was consecrated as bishop by 'Eusebius and the bishops with him'. Eusebius was one of the most eminent and influential churchmen of his day, and he was an Arian. In the last years of Constantine he was still bishop of Nicomedia and did not become bishop of Constantinople until 338, the year after Constantine died. It would seem to follow, therefore, that Ulfila was consecrated before 22 May 337, the date of Constantine's death, when

[1] See p. 81 n. 1 below. For the doubts, none of them persuasive, which have been thrown on Philostorgius here see (in English) C. A. A. Scott, *Ulfilas, Apostle of the Goths* (Cambridge, 1885), 50 f., followed by A. G. Hopkins, 'Ulfilas and the Conversion of the Goths', *The Andover Review*, xviii (1892), 162–79, at 165 f. Sadagolthina: S. Salaville, 'Un ancien bourg de Cappadoce', *Échos d'Orient*, xv (1912), 61–3. The site of Parnassus was identified by J. G. C. Anderson, *JHS*, xix (1899), 107–9.
[2] At any rate, Catholic Goths in Constantinople sang the Psalms in Gothic: John Chrysostom, *Homilies* ii and viii (Migne, *PG* lxiii. 472, 499), though it is not quite certain that τῇ βαρβάρων in the former sermon is a reference to Gothic—it is doubted e.g. by J. Mühlau, *Zur Frage nach d. gotischen Psalmenübersetzung*, Diss. Kiel, 1904, 15–8.

Eusebius still occupied the see of Nicomedia. Unfortunately, this conclusion conflicts with the evidence of
Auxentius. For Auxentius speaks no fewer than three
times of the 'forty years' of his master's bishopric;[1] and
since Ulfila died sometime in the period 381–3, this
figure of 'forty years' would be wrong by at least four
years and perhaps by as many as six, if he was appointed in 337. But it is far from certain that we can
assume such a degree of inaccuracy on the part of
Auxentius: he and Maximinus, who quotes him, wrote
in a highly controversial style for publication, and it
has been pointed out that they would scarcely have
given critical readers so easy an opening for attack as
an incorrect chronology.[2]

Various suggestions have been put forward to avoid
the difficulty. It is often thought that Philostorgius (or
the Byzantine bishop Photius who paraphrased him)
was guilty of a slip and that he wrote 'Constantine'
when in fact he meant Constantius II, who succeeded
his father in May 337. Others think that Ulfila travelled
twice in these years to the Roman Empire, once before
Constantine died in 337, and again when Eusebius was
bishop of Constantinople in 338–41, and that Philostorgius has conflated the two visits into one. Yet
another view is that Ulfila's embassy does indeed date
from before Constantine's death in 337, but that, while
the other envoys returned home when their business
was done, Ulfila remained in the Empire and was only

---

[1] Auxentius, 74. 35, 75. 35 and 38.
[2] So H. Giesecke, *Die Ostgermanen und der Arianismus* (Leipzig and
Berlin, 1939), 10 n. 17. I have rejected the revised chronology of Ulfila's
life proposed by D. B. Capelle, 'La lettre d'Auxence sur Ulfila', *RB*,
xxxiv (1922), 224–33: see J. Zeiller, 'Le premier établissement des Goths
chrétiens dans l'empire d'Orient', *Mélanges G. Schlumberger* (Paris, 1924),
i. 3–11.

consecrated after Constantine was dead and Eusebius had been translated to Constantinople.

Those who believe that Ulfila was appointed in the early years of Constantius II observe that, according to Philostorgius, Eusebius was accompanied by other bishops when he consecrated him. From this the inference is drawn that Ulfila was consecrated when a church synod was in progress; and since a well known synod was held at Antioch in 341, it is commonly believed that Ulfila was appointed at Antioch in that year. But this does not follow. When Eusebius was bishop, whether of Nicomedia or of Constantinople, he was the most energetic champion of Arianism of his day, and so he will have been visited often by other bishops and groups of bishops. Hence, Philostorgius' phrase, 'Eusebius and the bishops with him', by no means necessarily implies a synod.[1] And if it does imply a synod, it does not necessarily imply the synod of Antioch, for other synods may well have met in these years without any record of them having reached us.

It is clear that every opinion on the date of Ulfila's consecration involves jettisoning some of the evidence so that no choice between the conflicting views can be made with assurance. I am inclined to accept what Philostorgius says and to believe that Ulfila became bishop when Constantine was still alive, having been consecrated by Eusebius when Eusebius was still bishop of Nicomedia. And if it is asked why an envoy who presumably went to the capital was not consecrated by the bishop of the capital, the answer is that Paul, the last bishop of Constantinople in Constantine's reign, was a Nicaean, and hence would scarcely have felt inclined to promote a barbarian whom he would

[1] So Kaufmann, art. cit., 220.

have regarded as heretical. As for Auxentius, we may assume that he has rounded off the figures, and, although he is writing controversially, no controversial matter depends on their precise accuracy.

The exact date of Ulfila's consecration is a comparative detail. What is important is the fact that he was consecrated, not in order to convert his fellow-barbarians, but, as Philostorgius says explicitly, so as to serve as bishop to those Christians who were already living in Gothia. It seems to have been the Church's practice to send a bishop to serve outside the Roman frontier only when a request for one had been made by the community in question and only when the community had been consulted on the appointment. At any rate, that was the practice in the early fifth century, and there is no reason to think that it was an innovation then. Throughout the whole period of the Roman Empire not a single example is known of a man who was appointed bishop with the specific task of going beyond the frontier to a wholly pagan region in order to convert the barbarians living there. If there was no Christian community beyond the relevant frontier, then no bishop was sent there. From this it follows that as early as 341—let us accept the traditional date of Ulfila's consecration—there existed among the Visigoths a Christian community which was sufficiently organized to make known to Constantinople that it required the services of a bishop. Moreover, the ecclesiastical authorities in the capital recognized it to the extent that they consulted it on the appointment. But it does not follow that this Christian community in Gothia was composed mainly of Visigoths. It was composed for the most part of Christian prisoners, or the descendants of Christian prisoners, whom Gothic raiders had carried off from the Imperial provinces. The extent to which the Visigoths themselves had been converted in the mid-fourth century is a question that will face us later on.

For seven years after 341 Ulfila laboured in Gothia. No doubt he devoted much of his energy to explaining and defining to his flock the doctrines of Arius as he understood them and to refuting the objections which had been raised against them.[1] But, like St. Patrick in Ireland at a later date, he did not restrict his activities to those who were already converted. Indeed, his first converts, for all we know, may have been made even earlier than 341; for if the Christians in Gothia had already suggested his name to Eusebius as a suitable candidate for the bishopric, he must have made a considerable impact on his fellow-Christians even before his consecration. However that may be, after seven years there arose in Gothia 'an impious and sacriligious' chieftain, as Auxentius calls him,[2] and there followed, for reasons which are wholly unknown, the first persecution of the Christians in that country. It resulted in the death of many men and women, but Ulfila and a great throng of his followers managed to escape to the Roman provinces, and there is no evidence that he ever returned to Gothia north of the Danube. He was welcomed into the Empire by Constantius II (p. 97 below), and his headquarters henceforward were in a mountainous region near the city of Nicopolis in the province of Moesia Inferior

---

[1] Is this the meaning of Auxentius, 75. 19 'cristianos vere cristianos esse manifestavit et multiplicavit'?

[2] Auxentius, 75. 21 'ab inreligioso et sacrilego iudice Gothorum tyrannico terrore in varbarico cristianorum persecutio est excitata'. On the term *iudex* see pp. 44 ff. below.

(modern Trnovo in Bulgaria).[1] When Jordanes wrote his history of the Goths two hundred years later there still existed in the neighbourhood of Nicopolis a large but poor and unwarlike community, living on its flocks and herds. These were the descendants of Ulfila's followers.[2]

He continued as bishop—the title of his see is unknown—for thirty-three years after his return to the Roman Empire and he attended many councils of the Church.[3] But he appears specifically in history on only two further occasions; and on each of these we find him deeply involved in the theological controversies of his time. Early in 360 he was present at the Council of Constantinople, where the assembled bishops confirmed the formula drawn up by the Council of Rimini in the previous year and declared the Son to be 'like' (*homoios*) the Father—not 'of the same essence' or 'the one essence' with the Father, as the Council of Nicaea had declared. Indeed, they pronounced the word 'essence' (*ousia*) to be un-Scriptural and the cause of trouble to the people, and forbade its use. The word 'substance' (*hypostasis*), too, must never be mentioned. In discussing the relations of the Son and the Father, therefore, one could not say that they are 'of the same essence' or 'of the same substance'. The term to use is 'like': the Son is 'like' the Father. Of this curiously indefinite formula Duchesne has written: 'It is the official formulary of what was henceforth known as Arianism, in particular of that Arianism which spread itself among the barbarian peoples. . . . The vagueness of the formula allowed it to be understood in the most different and even the most directly opposite senses:

---

[1] Auxentius, loc. cit.; Philostorgius, ii. 5; Jordanes, *Get.* li. 267.
[2] Jordanes, loc. cit.   [3] Auxentius, 73. 40.

with a little complaisance, Athanasius and Aetius might have repeated it together. This is why it was so perfidious and so useless, and why no Christian worthy of the name ... could hesitate for a moment to condemn it.'[1] But it satisfied Ulfila: he was a Homoean.

Throughout the period of his bishopric the Roman Emperors, with a short interval in the years 361–4 (the reigns of Julian and Jovian), were favourable to Arianism. In particular, Valens (364–78) strongly supported the formula of Rimini and was a fervent Homoean like Ulfila. But at the very end of Ulfila's life conditions changed. On 27 February 380 Theodosius I issued his first law against heresy, enjoining all his subjects (though without as yet specifying penalties) to accept the faith of Damasus, bishop of Rome, and of Peter, bishop of Alexandria, both of whom supported the formulations of the Council of Nicaea.[2] He deposed Demophilus, the Arian bishop of Constantinople, and replaced him by the orthodox Gregory of Nazianzus.[3] On 10 January 381 he confiscated all churches belonging to heretics and handed them over to the Catholics: all religious meetings of heretics were banned.[4] (Whether he was strong enough to enforce these measures among the Visigothic communities of Moesia may be doubted.) In May he held the Second Ecumenical Council at Constantinople to define the official faith, and on 3 July he repeated his enactment on the handing over of the churches to the Nicaeans.[5] In the West, the Council of Aquileia in September of the same year deposed and anathematized two Arian bishops, Palladius of Ratiaria (Artscher in Bulgaria on the

[1] L. Duchesne, *Early History of the Christian Church* (London, 1950), ii. 244 f.
[2] *Cod. Theod.* xvi. 1. 2.   [3] Socrates, v. 7; Sozomen, vii. 5.
[4] *Cod. Theod.* xvi. 5. 6.   [5] Ibid., xvi. 1. 3.

bend of the Danube south of Vidin) and Secundinus of Singidunum (Belgrade); and we catch a glimpse of Ulfila travelling to Constantinople in the company of these two men in order to meet Theodosius.[1]

The incident is referred to in a passage of Auxentius where much of the manuscript text has become illegible, and hence the course of events cannot be reconstructed with any certainty.[2] If some words in the passage have been restored correctly, Ulfila was ordered by Theodosius to go to the capital to a 'disputation' (or 'council', as it is called later). Unhappily, the name of those with whom he was to dispute has proved impossible to restore. The fragmentary text shows that on reaching the city he found that the Catholics had altered the status of the council, apparently in such a way as to prevent Ulfila and his associates from expressing their views freely. While in the capital he fell ill and died, possibly at the end of 381, more probably in 382 or 383.[3]

Before dying he pronounced the creed which Auxentius has preserved for us. In his creed Ulfila asserts his belief in the unbegotten and invisible God, in His only begotten Son who created all, and in the Holy Spirit, who is neither God nor Lord, but the faithful servant of Christ, not equal to Him, but subject and obedient to the Son in all things even as the Son is subject and obedient in all things to the Father.

Auxentius elaborates his master's beliefs. He constantly preached of the one eternal God, who originally existed alone. It was He who created the Son, the only begotten God. This second God was the author of all

---

[1] Auxentius, 73. 10 f.
[2] Auxentius, 75. 38 ff. See the discussion of this capital text in K. K. Klein, *ZfdA*, lxxxiv (1952–3), 120; but Klein's reconstruction of Ulfila's last year or two is very hazardous.
[3] For the literature on the date of Ulfila's death see ibid., 101 f.

things, and regarded His Father as greater than He, a matter in which Ulfila 'despised and trampled upon the odious and execrable, depraved and perverse profession of the Homousians [the Nicaeans], as a diabolical invention and the doctrine of demons'.[1] In his sermons and tracts he constantly expounded the difference between the divinity of the Unbegotten God and that of the Only Begotten God: the Father was the creator of the Creator, and the Son was the creator of all creation. The Holy Spirit is neither the Father nor the Son, but was made by the Father through the Son before anything else was created. He is neither unbegotten nor begotten but was created by the Ungotten through the Only Begotten in the third grade. He cannot be called God or Lord. He is the servant of Christ. In the opinion of Ulfila and also of the Emperor Valens there was a clear separation and gradation of the three members of the Trinity.

We do not know when Ulfila translated the Bible; but this vast undertaking may well have occupied the entire forty years of his bishopric. Our authorities agree in saying that he had to begin his task by providing the Goths with an alphabet (p. 32 n. 1 below); and only when he had devised his alphabet and made his followers familiar with it can he have begun his enormous task.[2] Philostorgius says that he deliberately refrained from translating the Books of Kings owing to their warlike subject-matter: in this connexion the Goths 'needed the bridle' rather than the spur. But whether this is true is unknown, for practically the

---

[1] Auxentius, 73. 34 f.

[2] For the view that the Visigoths already had an alphabet, other than the runic, before Ulfila's time see S. Gutenbrunner, 'Ueber den Ursprung des gotischen Alphabets', *Beiträge*, lxxii (1950), 500–8; J. W. Marchand, 'Hatten die Goten vor Wulfila eine Schrift?', ibid., lxxxi (1959), 295 ff.

whole of his translation of the Old Testament is lost, and it has even been denied that he translated the Old Testament at all.

Almost all our knowledge of his Bible is derived from the surviving fragment of the famous Codex Argenteus. But this great manuscript is not a Visigothic work: it was written in Ulfila's alphabet in the Ostrogothic kingdom of Italy some time in the first half of the sixth century. The manuscript owes its name to the fact that it is written in silver ink on leaves of purple parchment. What became of it in the thousand years that followed upon the destruction of the Ostrogothic kingdom by the armies of Justinian is unknown. It first reappeared in the monastery of Werden on the river Ruhr near Essen in the middle of the sixteenth century. After a short stay in Prague, it fell into the hands of the Swedes, who entered that city in 1648, and was taken to Stockholm, where it was used to pay off some of Queen Christina's debts in 1654; and so the manuscript went to Holland, where it was first printed in 1665. But a Swedish nobleman, Count Magnus Gabriel De la Gardie, had already bought it before the printed edition appeared, and in 1669 he presented it to Uppsala University, in the Library of which it still lies, a splendid and moving sight.

CHAPTER ONE

POLITICAL HISTORY TO A.D. 395

ACCORDING to a Goth of the sixth century, southern Scandinavia was, so to speak, a workshop where peoples were made, the womb from which nations had sprung. From here the Gothic peoples set out in three ships under the leadership of one Berig and crossed to the southern Baltic coast. As soon as they landed they called the place *Gothiscandza*, 'the Gothic shore',[1] and the name was said to be still in use in the middle of the sixth century. But one of the three ships made the voyage slowly, and so a name was given to those who sailed in her; for the name of the Gepids had originally meant the 'slothful' or 'tardy', and an apt name it was, according to our Goth, for the Gepids are slow-moving folk of ponderous wit, unlike the vivacious Goths.[2] If this tale means to imply that the other two ships carried the Ostrogoths and the Visigoths respectively it is perhaps misleading, for these two great branches of the Goths do not appear to have separated and become distinguished from one another until they were settled in the Black Sea region. But nonetheless the story preserves the echo of some historical facts—the original home of the Gothic peoples in southern Scandinavia, their migration to the lands around the mouths of the Vistula, the close kinship of the Goths with the Gepids,

---

[1] On the name see S. Feist, *Vergleichendes Wörterbuch der gotischen Sprache*[3] (Leyden, 1939), 217 f., with references.

[2] Jordanes, *Get.* iv. 25, xvii. 95, cf. 99 *vivacitas ingenii*, though *vivacitas ingenii* is not a noticeable characteristic of Jordanes himself. Procopius, *BV* iii. 2. 5, says that the Gepid language was indistinguishable from Gothic.

I

and their antipathy to them. The Goths were in their
new homes on the Continent by the beginning of the
Christian era, and the Romans knew of their presence
there during the first century A.D.

Other Germanic peoples had reached the Vistula
area before them. The peoples collectively known as the
Vandals had been the first to come, then the Rugi and
the Burgundians. These the Gothic peoples fought and
conquered. But under Filimer, Gadaric's son, the fifth
king to reign after Berig, the Goths moved away, we are
told, to the south-east to the fertile lands north of the
Black Sea; and the story of their adventures on the way
and of their victories after they had arrived were
remembered in songs sung hundreds of years later.[1]
Early in the third century they were settled in the
Pontic region, and in 238 at latest came the first Gothic
attack on the Roman provinces. As the Empire seemed
to disintegrate in the middle of the third century the
Goths launched their vast raids into the provinces of
Asia Minor and of the Balkan peninsula, raids which
extended their geographical horizon until it came to
include Syria in the east and Dalmatia in the west and
Athens in the south.[2] The name of the Goths became
known even to the Parthians, though the Parthians
may not have been very clear as to what a Goth was, or

[1] Jordanes, *Get.* iv. 26 ff., xvii. 97 (Burgundians). It has been claimed
that their settlements on both sides of the lower Vistula, their expulsion
of the peoples living west of the Vistula delta, and their further settlements on the lower reaches of the Oder can all be traced in the archaeological record: see E. Blume, *Die germanischen Stämme und die Kulturen
zwischen Oder und Passarge*, Mannus-Bibliothek, no. 8 (Würzburg, 1912),
153, ff., a book which has had perhaps an undue influence. The claims
are premature: see C. Engel and W. La Baume, *Kulturen und Völker der
Frühzeit im Preussenland* (Königsberg, 1937), 137 f. The latest discussion
accessible to me is that of R. Schindler, *Die Besiedlungsgeschichte der Goten
und Gepiden im unteren Weichselraum* (Leipzig, 1940), esp. 97 ff., which also
seems hazardous.

[2] W. Schulze, *Kleine Schriften* (Göttingen, 1934), 533 f.

2

at any rate where the Goths lived.[1] At length Gothic pressure on the exposed province of Dacia (approximately Rumania) became so severe that, when the Emperor Aurelian (270–5) withdrew the legions from Dacia early in the seventies, Visigothic settlers began a general movement into the abandoned province.[2]

1. The Settlement in Dacia

The archaeological evidence, such as it is, suggests that their settlements were comparatively dense in the rich and fertile valley of the upper river Mures, from which they had easy access to the most important strategical points in the rest of Transylvania and where they could control the approaches from the Moldavian and Wallachian plains, which they also held.[3] Indeed, a map of Germanic objects hitherto found in Transylvania suggests that the Visigothic settlements were in nearly all cases close to the great rivers of their new country.[4]

To the south and south-east of them lay the crumbling fortifications and dispirited garrisons of the Romans along the line of the Danube, which Romans now sometimes called the 'Gothic bank' of the river, the *ripa*

[1] The so-called *Res Gestae Divi Saporis* seems to mean by ἔθνη Γούθθων Roman troops from the Danubian provinces: so M. Rostovtzeff, *Berytus*, viii (1943), 22, n. 13, who points out that the document provides no certain evidence that large numbers of Goths fought for Gordian in 243. The inscription gives the Parthian form of their name, *Gut* or *Gūt*: H. Junker, 'Der Gotenname bei Persepolis', *Beiträge*, lxxiv (1952), 296–9.
[2] On coin hoards found in Trajan's Dacia, which were buried as the Visigoths subjugated the country, see M. Macrea, 'Monetele și Părăsirea Daciei', *Anuarul Institutului de Studii Classice*, iii (1936–40), 271–305, at 283, 286, n. 2. On the question of the date of the evacuation of Dacia see C. Daicoviciu, *La Transylvanie dans l'antiquité* (Bucharest, 1945), 165–87, with bibliography.
[3] E. Beninger, 'Ein westgotisches Brandgrab von Maros-Lekencze (Siebenbürgen)', *Mannus*, xxx (1938), 122–41, at 122, 127.
[4] See the map in K. Horedt, 'Frühgeschichtliche Funde aus Siebenbürgen', *Deutsche Forschung im Südosten*, i (1942), 33–42, at 42.

3

Gothica.[1] The eastern limit of their territory was formed by the northward curve of the Danube and by the Black Sea coast, on which they had a small port (p. 29 below). Towards the north-east their land extended as far as the Dniester, but there is no means of saying how far north along the river their frontier ran.[2] Beyond the Dniester the Ostrogoths controlled a huge empire in the Ukraine. The western and northern limits of Gothia cannot be determined exactly, but in spite of the occupation of eastern Transylvania the Visigoths fell far short of the Tisza and do not seem to have reached the present Hungarian-Rumanian border: perhaps the Bihor or the Apuseui mountains formed their western border. In a word, the Visigoths occupied Bessarabia, Muntenia, and Moldavia together with eastern and central Transylvania.[3]

In addition to the Romans and the Ostrogoths in the south and north-east respectively, their neighbours also included the 'slothful' Gepids in the mountains north of Transylvania, the Vandals directly to the west, the Sarmatians (a non-Germanic people) in the Banat, and a somewhat mysterious people of whom we know little called the Taifali in Oltenia.[4]

When they entered Dacia the Visigoths did not enter a desolate and empty land. A number of Romano-Dacians had not left the country when Aurelian withdrew the legions and the administrative personnel from the

---

[1] Anon. Vales., 35. Further upstream was the *ripa Sarmatica*: Claudian, *Epithal. Pallad.* 88. On the Gothic name for the Danube see Pseudo-Caesarius of Nazianzus, *Dial.* i. 68 (Migne, *PG* xxxviii. 936) Δούναβις, iii. 144 (ibid., 1093) Δουναϋις (Müllenhoff, Δουναϋτις codd.).

[2] Amm. Marc., xxxi. 3. 3–7.

[3] For the occupation of Dacia see Eutropius, viii. 2; Orosius, i. 2. 53; Jordanes, *Get.* xii. 74.

[4] C. Patsch, 'Banater Sarmaten', *Anzeiger d. Akad. d. Wissen. in Wien: phil.-hist. Klasse*, lxii (1925), 189 f.; M. Fluss, P.-W. iv A. 2027.

province, but still continued to live there;[1] and urban life continued in an impoverished way in the ruined or decayed Roman cities until the sixth and seventh centuries. It is true that in the period from Aurelian's evacuation until the reign of Diocletian Roman coins seem to have failed almost completely to reach Gothia (though not the non-Visigothic Banat); and the reasons for this phenomenon, which has been observed in other frontier regions besides Gothia, are obscure.[2] It was not due to intense warfare on the lower Danube during the years in question (approximately 270–300), for that would not explain the appearance of a similar pheno-menon among other frontier barbarians at this time; and in fact the Visigoths remained at peace with Rome for a considerable period after they had moved into Dacia.[3] No doubt it was due to the collapse of the Imperial coinage in these years and to some extent also to the Visigoths' unfamiliarity with the use of money, for Roman coins had rarely reached them in the decades immediately before they entered Dacia, when they were still living in southern Russia.[4] However that may be, in the early fourth century coins reached Gothia in great numbers and have been found very often on the sites of the old Roman settlements, both civil and military, including Porolissum, Napoca (Cluj), Potaissa (Turda), Micia, Cedonia, and the old Roman capital Sarmizegethusa, where faint traces in the archaeological

---

[1] On the whole question of the 'continuity' of the Rumanians see Daicoviciu, op. cit., 191 ff., with the bibliography in 191, n. 2.

[2] See e.g. E. Norden, *Alt-Germanien* (Leipzig and Berlin, 1934), 42–8, who does not, however, discuss the case of Gothia.

[3] Amm. Marc., xxxi. 5. 17.

[4] V. V. Kropotkin, 'Klady rimskich Monet v vostochnoi Evrope', *Vestnik Drevnei Istorii* (1951), 4. 243–81, at 248 f., with Tables 1–2. On the other hand, large numbers of Roman coins had reached the lower Vistula area in the early Imperial period: Engel and La Baume, op. cit., 158.

5

record, we are told, suggest that a humble life continued in the forum and the amphitheatre after Aurelian's evacuation.[1] There can be little doubt that a form of Roman life could still be found in all these and other places long after the Imperial administration and the legions were gone, especially in the non-Visigothic Banat and Oltenia, though by no means there alone.[2] But there is little evidence for city life among the Visigoths themselves. They lived in open villages,[3] and the accounts of Valens' campaigns in Gothia in 367–9 (p. 18 below) give no hint that they had any fortified places (though it might be argued on the other side that the Visigothic strategy on that occasion—a strategy of general withdrawal to the mountains and marshes before Valens' advancing army—would not give our authorities much reason to mention fortified places even if the Visigoths had possessed them). But if we deny the existence of urban life among the fourth-century Visigoths, we cannot deny that their villages

[1] Daicoviciu, op. cit., 233.

[2] Full bibliography and discussion of the coin evidence in Macrea, art. cit., 300 f. On Sarmizegethusa see J. Jung, 'Zur Geschichte der Pässe Siebenbürgens', *Mittheilungen d. Instituts f. österreichische Geschichtsforschung*, iv Ergänzungsband (1893), 1–31, at 13, n. 6. 17, n. 3; Daicoviciu, op. cit., 233 ff. For a find of coins (Trajan-Diocletian) at a site near Sighişoara see K. Horedt, 'Völkerwanderungszeitliche Funde aus Siebenbürgen', *Germania*, xxv (1941), 121–6, at 123, and for what may be archaeological evidence for a continuation of Roman life at Apulum (Alba Iulia) in Visigothic times see idem, 'Funde der Völkerwanderungszeit aus Siebenbürgen', *Anuarul Institutului de Studii Classice*, iv (1941–4), 163–79, at 165.

[3] *Passion of St. Saba*, 218. 2 and 4, 219. 4. The *polis* of ibid., 218. 18, is identical with the *kome* mentioned there, though J. Mansion, 'Les origines du Christianisme chez les Gots', *Analecta Bollandiana*, xxxiii (1914), 5–30, at 6, followed by K. Horedt, 'Eine lateinische Inschrift des 4. Jahrhunderts aus Siebenbürgen', *Anuarul* (as above), iv (1941–4), 10–17, at 15, thinks that it was an old Roman town which had continued in existence before the Visigothic invasion. We know nothing of the 'oppidum Galtis, iuxta quod currit fluvius Auha', Jordanes, *Get.* xvii. 99. For an attempt to identify it see Feist, op. cit., s.v., who is inclined to think (s.v. *ahva*) that Auha is simply the Gothic *ahva = aqua*.

6

may have been sizable and thronged with buyers and sellers at market-time.

When we turn to the native rural population of Gothia we are confronted with a problem of extreme obscurity. But a cemetery has been excavated in the county of Poieneşti, twenty kilometres west of Vaslui in Moldavia, and a little light has been thrown into the darkness. The cemetery was in use at the end of the third century and throughout the greater part of the fourth. The finds include brooches of bronze and iron, mostly of the type 'with returned foot', which were made by Goths or under Gothic influence; but side by side with these were brooches of contemporary provincial Roman types. There were also glass bottles with decoration in relief, datable to the fourth century, which had been imported from the Empire. No coins were found in the burial urns, but a few were discovered elsewhere in the cemetery—three bronze coins of the mid-third century and a silver one of Constantius II (337–61). At first sight it is tempting to regard this cemetery as Visigothic, more especially as the people who used it were newcomers in the late third century and had disappeared before the opening of the fifth. But in spite of the brooches 'with returned foot' the excavators found little or nothing which could be considered as proving that those who used the cemetery were Germans; and I would suggest that the overwhelming predominance of cremation tells decisively against their having been Visigoths.[1] It may seem,

[1] For details of the excavation see R. Vulpe and others, *Studii şi Cercetări de Istorie Veche*, i (1950), 41–46. The only Visigothic cremation-grave hitherto found is that excavated at Lechinţa de Mureş in Transylvania: see Beninger, art. cit., 128 f. All the bodies in the cemetery excavated at Sântana de Mureş and Târgu Mureş (p. 34 f. below) had been interred, whereas the majority of the Ostrogoths buried in the cemeteries found near Kiev had been cremated. Cremation disappeared

7

then, that here we have a community of people who were subject to the Visigoths or, more probably, lived side by side with them; and it is noteworthy not only that some of their ornaments were influenced, if not made, by Goths but also that they traded with the Roman provinces. The Visigothic occupation had not cut off this community from contact with the Empire. Beyond that we can only say that village life still continued in Wallachia in the middle of the fifth century. Indeed, in some parts of Wallachia there would seem to have been a considerable density of population, for a traveller who went there in 449 passed through several villages in the course of a single day's journey; and it can scarcely be doubted that these villages were inhabited in the main by the old Roman population.[1] It may be that the revival of the use of money in Dacia at the beginning of the fourth century was due primarily to the Romano-Dacian population of the ruined cities, who then proceeded to introduce it to the Visigoths.[2] Indeed, it has been argued that some of the pottery found at Sântana de Mures (p. 34 f. below) shows a blending of Roman and even pre-Roman with Germanic styles; and it has accordingly been concluded that the Visigoths and Romano-Dacians were living side by side in this area in the early fourth century and were making common use of the potteries.[3] It must be so completely from among the Visigoths and Burgundians that the law-codes of those two peoples never have occasion to lay down a penalty for it or even to mention it.

[1] Priscus of Panium, frag. 8 (321. 1, ed. Dindorf), cf. 300. 15 ff., 301. 22, 303. 15, 320. 29. That Priscus' journey led him through Wallachia has been shown by R. Browning, 'Where was Attila's Camp?', *JHS*, lxxiii (1953), 143–5.

[2] So Macrea, art. cit., 299.

[3] Daicoviciu, op. cit., 247 f.; Kovacs in the first of the two articles cited on p. 35 n. 3 below. *Contra*, E. Brenner, 'Der Stand der Forschung über die Kultur der Merowingerzeit', *VII Bericht der röm.-german. Kommission* (1912), 253–351, at 266.

admitted, however, that all this is highly speculative, and we can scarcely be said to know what the value or significance may have been of the first peaceful contacts of the invaders with the Roman survivors.

These, then, were the lands and the environment of the Visigothic people, *Gutthiuda*, as they called themselves,[1] when they had moved into the old Roman province of Dacia. Here they lived for exactly a century until in 376 the Huns fell upon them, and they were sent fleeing across the *ripa Gothica* into the fertile fields of Thrace.

2. *Constantine and Constantius II*

After they had occupied Dacia, the Visigoths refrained for a generation or two from seriously molesting the Roman Empire (p. 5 above). No doubt they were busy digesting their conquests, but no information has reached us on the way in which they settled on the land. We do not know how they decided where each 'tribe' should live or whether in fact any formal decision was taken: perhaps each group settled down in whatever district the impetus of the invasion had carried them to. It is true that we hear of occasional raids on the Roman provinces, but they probably amounted to little; and we also hear of border wars with their barbarian neighbours, the Vandals, the Gepids, and the Sarmatians.[2] One of the chieftains who fell through a trick or an ambush of the Sarmatians, Vidigoia by name, was still remembered generations later in the

[1] R. Loewe, 'Der gotische Kalender', *ZfdA*, lix (1922), 245–90, at 247–9; cf. P. Kretschmer, 'Austria und Neustria', *Glotta*, xxvi (1938), 207–40, at 212.
[2] *Paneg. Lat.* (ed. E. Galletier), iii (xi). 17 'Tervingi, pars alia Gothorum, adiuncta manu Taifalorum, adversum Vandalos Gipedesque concurrunt', iv (viii). 10 'summittente se Gotho pace poscenda'; Jordanes, *Get.* xxii. 113 ff. (Vandals), etc.

songs which the Visigoths sang to the strains of the harp.[1]

In 315, however, during the joint reign of Constantine the Great and Licinius, there seems to have been a greater disturbance than usual on the lower Danube; and the Romans strengthened the fortifications of the frontier there.[2] Much more serious trouble came in 323. The frontier defence forces were largely removed from the lower Danube by Constantine, now engaged in his final and vast campaign against his rival, the Emperor Licinius. The Visigoths used their opportunity to the full, and heavily attacked the provinces of Scythia, Thrace, and Moesia.[3] Before long, however, Constantine was able to drive them back across the frontier and force them to surrender their prisoners.[4] But he gave them the status of Federates: that is, in return for annual subsidies they were obliged to defend the Roman frontier against attacks by other barbarians.

But the Emperor evidently had little confidence in his new Federates; and in 328 he built a stone bridge across the Danube some four kilometres south-west of the modern Corabia between Oescus (near the village of Gigen in Bulgaria) and Sucidava (Celeiu in Rumania),[5] and himself crossed the river several times in the

[1] Jordanes, *Get.* v. 43, xxxiv. 178. On the site of Vidigoia's death see Browning, art. cit., 144 f.

[2] O. Fiebiger and L. Schmidt, *Inschriftensammlung zur Geschichte der Ostgermanen*, Denkschriften d. kais. Akademie d. Wissen. in Wien: phil.-hist. Klasse, Bd. 60, Abh. 3 (Vienna, 1917), nos. 160–61 = Dessau, *ILS* 8938, 695.

[3] John Lydus, *de Mag.* ii. 10, iii. 31 and 40, with *Hermes*, lxxxiv (1956), 378 f.

[4] Anon. Vales., 21; cf. Zonaras, xiii. 2 *fin.* The Sarmatian war described in Zosimus, ii. 21, did not concern the Goths: see L. Schmidt, *Ungarische Jahrbücher*, v (1925), 114 f., though there is no reason to suppose that Rausimod himself (mentioned by Zosimus there) was a Goth.

[5] Chron. Pasch. in Mommsen, *Chron. Min.* i. 233, s.a. 328; Aur. Victor, *Caes.* xli. 18 'pons per Danubium ductus; castra castellaque pluribus locis commode posita'; idem, *Epit.* xli. 14; Theophanes, xxviii.

period when the bridge was being built.[1] The bridge debouched into the extreme south-eastern corner of Oltenia, that is, into territory occupied not by the Visigoths but by the Taifali. Moreover, he drove a road northwards from his bridge, presumably as far as Romula (Reşca on the Olt); and of this road one milestone has been discovered. Now, the bridge and the road were not designed for the use of traders, sightseers, and Gothic mercenaries: the fact is that in 328 the Emperor reoccupied a part of the old province of Dacia, which Aurelian had evacuated some sixty years before. This reoccupied land was Oltenia, or at any rate some territory on the lower Olt,[2] and it entailed the conquest of the Taifali. It is probably with this event that we must associate the presence of Taifali in Phrygia: it would seem that after his conquest Constantine transported a number of this people to Asia Minor, where they are known to have rebelled in the course of his reign.[3] The reoccupation of part of

19 ff. (= Cedrenus, i. 517. 23 f., ed. Bonn). See also C. Schuchhardt, *Archaeol.-epigraph. Mitteil.* ix (1885), 229 f.; A. Alföldi, *Zeitschrift für Numismatik*, xxxvi (1926), 161–74. The *castra castellaque* mentioned by Aur. Victor are not said to have been on the Danube, and so I do not revert to them.

[1] Chron. Pasch., loc. cit.

[2] D. Tudor, 'Ein konstantinischer Meilenstein in Dazien', *Serta Hoffilleriana* (Zagreb, 1940), 241–7, who supposes, ibid., 246, that Constantine occupied most of the Wallachian plain. Tudor has also set out his views in 'Constantin cel Mare şi Recucerirea Daciei Traiane', *Rivista Istorică Română*, xi–xii (1941–2), 134–48, with references to further Rumanian literature.

[3] *Vita S. Nicolai*, xvii, xx (Migne, *PG* cxvi. 337, 341). For another and less likely view see C. Patsch, 'Beiträge zur Völkerkunde von Südosteuropa, III', *Sitzungsberichte d. Akad. d. Wissen. in Wien: phil.-hist. Klasse*, Bd. ccviii, Abh. 2 (1928), 30, who connects the Taifali in Asia with the raid mentioned in Zosimus, ii. 31. 3. But the Taifali in Asia were clearly a strong force, whereas that raid was a small affair carried out by 500 men and is not said to have been unsuccessful. L. Schmidt, *Geschichte der deutschen Stämme: die Ostgermanen* (Munich, 1934), 227, supposes that the Taifali were defeated and sent to Phrygia in 332; but a conquest of Oltenia in 332 is unlikely.

11

Dacia is mentioned by several ancient writers,[1] and its value was seen in 332.

In that year the Visigoths began yet another of their wars against the Sarmatians in the Banat; but this time the Sarmatians appealed to Constantine for help. The Emperor evidently hoped to consolidate his new conquest, for he came to the Sarmatians' aid, though it was an event of great rarity in Imperial history for the Romans to intervene in force in a war between barbarian and barbarian beyond the northern frontier (except when they had already decided to push the frontier forward and were merely looking for an excuse to do so). Having a foothold across the Danube, Constantine was able to send an army led by his son Constantine II from Oltenia to take the Visigoths in the rear; and the result was a shattering defeat of the Goths. The Romans claimed, doubtless with some exaggeration, that no less than 100,000 Visigoths were killed by hunger or exposure; and hostages were taken from them, one of whom was the son of the 'king' (rex) Ariaric.[2] Moreover, Constantine stopped the payment of subsidies to them: he no longer required Federates in Wallachia, since he now had a bridgehead across the Danube and his own troops could put a stop to barbarian invasions.[3]

---

[1] Eusebius, Vita Const. i. 8; Julian, Caes. 329 C; Theophanes and Cedrenus, locc. citt.

[2] Anon. Vales., 30; Chron. Min., i. 234, s. a. 332; Eusebius, Vita Const. iv. 5; Julian, Or. i. 9 D; Eutropius, x. 7; Jerome, Chron., s.a. 332; Orosius, vii. 28. 29; Sozomen, i. 8. 8 f.; cf. Dessau, ILS 820 with Addenda, iii. p. clxxii. For numismatical evidence see O. Seeck, Zeitschrift für Numismatik, xxi (1898), 35–8.

[3] Eusebius, Vita Const. iv. 5. This is not contradicted by Julian, Caes. 329 A, who does not specify the barbarians to whom he says that Constantine paid 'tribute': there is no reason to think that Julian has the Visigoths in mind, and, even if he has, he may be referring to the years before 332. Jordanes, Get. xxi. 111 f., relates (not without inaccuracy) to the period before 332, and the Visigoths were undoubtedly Federates in 323–32.

The fate of Constantine's reconquered territory in Dacia is very obscure. But when the Visigoths next reappear in political history, towards the year 367, the year of Valens' first attack on them, three striking changes had come about on the lower Danube. In the first place, the Romans now held no extensive territory north of the river. When Valens set about attacking the Visigoths in 367, his first move was to build a bridge of boats across the Danube at Daphne; and in 368, when the river was abnormally flooded, the Romans were not able to enter Gothia at all.[1] This position of stalemate would scarcely have been allowed to arise if the Emperor had been in a position to strike eastwards from Oltenia. Moreover, in Valens' time the Taifali were no longer subject to the Romans: as early as 358 we find that they are independent Federates, and it follows that in that year Oltenia was no longer Roman territory.[2]

Secondly, although Constantine after his victory in 332 stopped the payments of annual subsidies to the Visigoths, the Roman government was undoubtedly paying them in 364, when Valentinian and Valens ascended the throne;[3] and in 367 the Romans were making substantial payments of gold, silver, and clothing to them.[4] At that time they had long been the Federates of the Empire.[5] Indeed, after his victory in 369 Valens refused to make these payments any longer, just as Constantine had refused in 332. True, Visigothic raiding bands had often troubled the frontier districts of the Empire in the years preceding 367; but these bands seem to have been local or tribal levies, retinues

[1] Amm. Marc., xxvii. 5. 2 and 5 f.   [2] Idem, xvii. 13. 19 f.
[3] Themistius, *Or*. viii. 119 C.   [4] Idem, *Or*. x. 35 AB.
[5] Amm. Marc., xxvii. 5. 1, though there is no such indication in xxii. 7. 7.

13

of Gothic optimates, and so on.[1] They were not sent out by the central authority among the Visigoths, and their activities, though of course illegal,[2] were not inconsistent with the Federate status of the Visigoths as a whole

The third difference between the conditions of 332 and those of 367 is this. When Valens won the war of 367-9 he imposed restrictions on the activities of Visigothic traders: in future they would be allowed to trade at two only of the Roman frontier towns. But before the war they had been able to trade indiscriminately along the whole frontier. The phrase which our authority uses may mean 'in the days of peace before the war of 367', but it may also mean 'under the terms of the former peace-treaty'.[3] In the latter case the Visigoths had not acquired permission to trade in the Roman cities merely as a result of Roman indifference or generosity: they had secured it under the terms of a clause in a peace-treaty with the Roman government. In any case, the fact that the Gothic traders had had indiscriminate access to the Roman frontier towns before 367 is very remarkable. Since the earliest days of the Roman Empire the Imperial government had been reluctant to give unrestricted access to the traders of a hostile, or potentially hostile, barbarian people. True,

[1] Idem, xxii. 7. 7; xxvi. 4. 5 'praedatorii globi Gothorum'; Themistius, *Or.* x. 136 C κατὰ λόχους καὶ οὐλαμούς (cf. viii. 119 C); Zosimus, iv. 10. 1 μοίρας τῶν ὑπὲρ τὸν Ἴστρον Σκυθῶν τὰ Ῥωμαίων ὅρια ταραττούσης, i.e. part, but not all, of the Visigoths; cf. Seeck, *Untergang*, v. 588. On the other hand, the raids carried out on the Dobrogea in 337–40 (Dessau, *ILS* 724) were not the work of Federates. In 365 the Emperors ordered the construction of watch-towers on the frontier of Dacia Ripensis (*Cod. Theod.* xv. 1. 13); but unfortunately it is not clear whether these towers were to be erected on the part of the frontier facing the Taifali in Oltenia or on that facing the Sarmatians in the Banat.

[2] Cf. Amm. Marc., xix. 11. 5.

[3] Themistius, *Or.* x. 135 CD ἐπὶ τῆς προτέρας εἰρήνης.

the Hermunduri living north of Regensburg in Bavaria had been subject to no restrictions for a while in the first century A.D.; but their case was unique in the first century, and it is thought that they did not enjoy their freedom of entry for very long.[1] We have many references in ancient authors to the restrictions placed by the Roman authorities on visits by foreign traders,[2] and some words of Tacitus show that this was not a matter on which the government would show any laxity.[3] It can scarcely be doubted, then, that freedom to enter the market towns on the lower Danubian frontier was given to the Visigoths only with reluctance on the part of the Romans. The restriction imposed by Valens caused considerable loss to Roman as well as to Visigothic traders, for the trade had been a flourishing one.[4] But the government would hardly allow the interests of frontier traders to interfere with its frontier policy: the Visigoths were a powerful and dangerous people, and it is out of the question that Constantine

---

[1] Tacitus, *Germ.* xli. 1–2. (On the date to which Tacitus refers see Much's commentary, 364, with the works cited by him.) Cf. J. Klose, *Roms Klientel-Randstaaten am Rhein und an der Donau* (Breslau, 1934), 64 f., and the works there cited.

[2] Tacitus, *Hist.* iv. 64 f.; Dio Cassius, lxxi. 11. 3 and 15 (which shows that the Marcomanni had had unrestricted access to trading towns for a period in the second century), lxxii. 19. 2; Dessau, *ILS* 775, and for some new archaeological evidence see W. Schleiermacher, 'Nundinenses', *Germania*, xxxii (1954), 326–8, with references to further archaeological evidence. See also the conjectures of Patsch, art. cit. ('Banater Sarmaten'), 189. Some also cite Tertullian, *adv. Iud.* vii, but that passage has nothing to do with peace-time restrictions on crossing the frontier. References to restrictions on trade with Persia are frequent, e.g. Amm. Marc., xiv. 3. 3, xxiii. 3. 7; Peter the Patrician, frag. 14; *Cod. Justin.* iv. 63. 4; Menander Protector, frag. 11 (pp. 21 f., ed. Dindorf), etc.

[3] Tacitus, *Germ.* xli. 2. We must disagree, therefore, with Sir R. E. M. Wheeler, *Rome Beyond the Imperial Frontiers* (London, 1954), 9 f., who writes: 'Whatever the custom on the Rhine, traffic across the Danube frontier would appear to have been substantially unregulated until the disturbances of the latter half of the second century': that is not proved by Dio Cassius, lxxi. 15.

[4] Themistius, *Or.* x. 135 CD.

15

after his great victory in 332 would have allowed them unlimited access to the Danubian cities.

In the interval between the campaigns of Constantine and Valens, then, the Roman bridgehead across the lower Danube had been abandoned, the Visigoths had regained their status as Federates along with the payments of goods and money which that status entailed, and they had also secured, perhaps as a result of an explicit clause written into a treaty with the Romans, the unusual right to trade wherever they wished in the Roman frontier towns. These three facts suggest, I think, that the Romans had not abandoned their Transdanubian territory voluntarily: they had been beaten out of Oltenia and had made a most unfavourable peace-treaty with the Visigoths.

When did this war take place? It will hardly be thought that Constantine himself suffered a severe reverse on the Danube in 332–7. A major defeat of the great Emperor in his last years is unthinkable; and if he had been so defeated, the Visigoths would not have looked upon him with the deep respect which they are known to have felt for him.[1] As for the *terminus ante quem*, this is 353, for any major war on the Danube, if it had taken place after that year, would without question have been recorded by Ammianus Marcellinus, whose extant narrative opens with the events of 353. The Transdanubian territory, then, was lost between 337, when Constantine died, and 353, when Ammianus' narrative begins. Our sources for Roman political history in the years 337–353 are very meagre and broken. But we find hints in a speech of the orator Libanius delivered late in 348 or in 349 that a great invasion of the Empire was launched in wintertime by

[1] Eutropius, x. 7; John of Antioch, frag. 170.

16

the Goths, when the Danube was frozen over. The Emperor Constantius II, who was engaged with the Persians, 'persuaded' them to make peace and recognized them as Federates of the Empire.[1] It looks as though this was the war in which Oltenia was lost to the Romans and the bridge of Constantine broken down.[2] And it is most unfortunate that the date cannot be recovered, and that the connexion, if any, between this war and the first persecution of the Visigothic Christians is unknown.[3]

3. Valens and Theodosius I

The advisers of the Emperor Julian the Apostate suggested to him early in 363 that he would do better to attack the Visigoths, who were treacherous and unreliable Federates, than to assail the Persian Empire. But Julian rejected their advice, and marched to Persia on his last and fatal campaign (p. 40 below).

When Valentinian and his brother Valens began to reign in 364, it was clear that there would soon be trouble on the lower Danube. Plundering bands of Visigoths were raiding Thrace and Moesia on such a scale as to attract the attention of an historian.[4] These raids were sufficiently encouraging to the barbarians to cause them in the following year to federate their tribes, unify their command (p. 43 f. below), and plan to launch a full-scale invasion of Thrace. This state of affairs was reported by the frontier commanders to Valens, who was in Bithynia at the time on his way to

---

[1] Libanius, *Or.* lix. 89 f., with *Hermes*, lxxxiv (1956), 379–81.
[2] For other theories of how the bridge may have come to an end see Patsch, art. cit. ('Beiträge'), 44.
[3] For a guess see *Hermes*, loc. cit.
[4] Amm. Marc., xxvi. 4. 5, where the reading *Pannonias* is surely impossible.

17

Syria. He reinforced the points on the Danube where raids might be expected;[1] and the reinforcements of cavalry and infantry evidently deterred the Goths from carrying out their plan for the time being. Their leaders sent 3,000 men, however, to help the usurping Emperor Procopius; but in due course Valens forced these to surrender, disarmed them, and distributed them throughout the cities south of the Danube, where a watch was to be kept on them.[2]

The despatch of this force to help the usurper was used by Valens as a pretext for an attack on Gothia, the real purpose of which was to forestall a Gothic attack on the Empire.[3] The Emperor made careful preparations during the winter of 366–7;[4] and in 367, as we have seen (p. 13 above), he crossed the Danube at the fortress of Daphne on a bridge of boats which he built for the purpose. The Visigoths retired to the Transylvanian Alps before his advancing army, and the Emperor could do no more than capture a few stragglers who had failed to reach the mountains in time.[5] Some Goths who had taken refuge in the marshes of their country made small raids on the Roman army; but the Emperor offered a reward to any of his camp-followers who should bring in a Gothic head. His men scoured the woods and marshes, and many won the reward.[6] But the campaign as a whole achieved little.

In 368 the Danube was so extensively flooded that Valens could not cross it at all. In 369 he again made a bridge of boats, this time at Noviodunum, and entered Gothia for the second time. After long marches, during

---

[1] Idem, xxvi. 6. 11.
[2] Idem, xxvi. 10. 3; Zosimus, iv. 7. 2, 10. 1.
[3] Amm. Marc., xxvii. 4. 1, 5. 1, xxxi. 4. 13; Zosimus, iv. 10. 2 f.
[4] Zosimus, iv. 10. 4–11. 1.
[5] Amm. Marc., xxvii. 5. 2–4.　　[6] Zosimus, iv. 11. 2 f.

which he seems even to have had a brush with the Ostrogoths, he found Athanaric and the Visigoths ready, after some skirmishes, to face him in a pitched battle. The Emperor put them to flight and won a complete success.[1]

What was the reason for the Visigoths' disastrous change of strategy? We have an excellent contemporary authority for these campaigns, Ammianus Marcellinus, and he fortunately answers this question. He gives two reasons. First, the Emperor's long stay in Gothia unnerved them, and secondly, Valens broke off all trading relations with the Goths during the war so that the barbarians were reduced to hardship 'owing to their extreme lack of the necessities of life'. The privations caused by the ban on trade had forced them, even before the final battle, to send several embassies to the Romans asking for peace. It seems that an immediate end to the war and an immediate restoration of trading facilities had become essential if many of the Visigoths were not to perish of starvation.[2] Valens agreed to allow them to trade at two points on the frontier, but he no longer recognized them as Federates and he paid them no more subsidies.[3]

It would be of the utmost interest to know how the ban on trade with the Roman provinces could have had such an effect on Visigothic life. What foreign commodities did they need so desperately? We do not

---

[1] Amm. Marc., xxvii. 5. 6; Zosimus, iv. 10–11; cf. Eunapius, frag. 37 *fin.*; Fiebiger-Schmidt, *Inschriftensammlung*, no. 167. The fact that Themistius says nothing of the battle does not outweigh the fact that Ammianus *does* mention it.

[2] Amm. Marc., xxvii. 5. 7 'aderant post diversos triennii casus finiendi belli materiae tempestivae: prima quod ex principis diuturna permansione metus augebatur hostilis; dein quod conmerciis vetitis ultima necessariorum inopia barbari stringebantur'.

[3] Themistius, *Or.* x. 135 CD.

19

know; but the Romans knew, and they put their knowledge to use again in 414. In that year they blockaded the coast of Gallia Narbonensis, where the Visigoths were living at the time, and stringently forbade all sea-trade with them.[1] The Visigothic resistance to them collapsed dramatically and at once. They fled to Barcelona. The blockade was maintained in Spain, and the Visigoths were reduced to extreme famine conditions.[2] In vain they tried to cross over into Africa, and at last they capitulated in 416.[3] The great Visigothic invasion of the Roman Empire, which had begun in 376, had come to an ignominious end. These are facts which we cannot account for.

A curious incident took place during the final peace negotiations in 369. The Visigothic chief Athanaric declared that he was bound by a terrible oath and prohibited by his father's orders from ever setting foot on Roman soil. The Emperor felt it beneath his dignity in these circumstances to go once more to Gothia; and the two finally met on a boat in the middle of the Danube, and there the final conditions of peace were agreed.[4]

The defeat at Valens' hands was followed immediately by the second persecution of the Christians living in Gothia, and I shall suggest later on (p. 102 below) that this may not have been a coincidence: in some sense the persecution may have been an answer to the

---

[1] Orosius, vii. 43. 1 'interdicto praecipue atque intercluso omni commeatu navium et peregrinorum usu commerciorum'.

[2] Olympiodorus of Thebes, frag. 29. The name *truli* in this fragment is discussed by M. Vasmer, 'Ein vandalischer Name der Goten', *Studia Neophilologica*, xv (1942–3), 132–4.

[3] Olympiodorus, frag. 31; Orosius, vii. 43. 12 f.; *Chron. Min.* i. 468, s.a. 416; ii. 19, s.a. 416; Jordanes, *Get.* xxxii. 165 (who says nothing of the famine).

[4] Amm. Marc., xxvii. 5. 9 f.

defeat. Be that as it may, the persecution is not known to have continued after the year 372, and for the next four years little is known of the Visigoths. But in 376 a disaster of the first magnitude befell them.

Like the Greeks and Romans the Goths knew nothing about the origin of the Huns; but a story circulated among them which has been preserved by Jordanes.[1] According to this tale, there was once a Gothic chief called Filimer (p. 2 above) who ruled over his people in the fifth generation after they had left Scandinavia. Among his subjects he discovered certain witches, who were called in the Gothic language *Haliurunnae*. These he expelled from among his people and drove them into the solitude of the Scythian desert. Some evil spirits, who were wandering about the wilderness, saw these witches and fell upon them, so that they brought forth this most ferocious of all races, this race of quasi-men, the Huns.

Appearing in Europe *c.* 370 they quickly overran the great Ostrogothic empire of Ermanaric in the Ukraine and reached the Dniester, the frontier of the Visigoths. The Visigothic chief Athanaric determined to resist the new invaders if his people, too, should be attacked, and for this purpose he took up a position a short distance back from the banks of the Dniester. He began his operations by sending some of his chief men, led by Munderic, to report on the enemy's movements, while he himself prepared the main army for battle. But the Huns disregarded Munderic's scouting force, which had advanced some twenty miles. They rode hard through a moonlit night, forded the Dniester, and completely surprised and defeated Athanaric. The Visigothic chieftain next tried to defend himself by building walls

[1] Jordanes, *Get.* xxiv. 121 f.

21

between the rivers Prut and Danube, but while he was still busy with the work the Huns again surprised and again routed him. The Visigoths panicked. They had evidently been unable to get their harvest in and were now short of food. They deserted Athanaric and in the autumn of 376 appeared on the northern bank of the Danube begging the Romans to admit them to the security of the Imperial provinces.[1]

There is no need to retell the story of how the Romans starved them as they admitted them to the Empire or of the war which culminated on 9 August 378 in the battle of Adrianople, in which the Visigoths led by Fritigern defeated and killed the Emperor Valens. The extensive and confused fighting and devastation which laid waste the Danubian provinces in 378–82 cannot be described owing to the inadequacy of our sources of information.[2] But peace was eventually restored by the treaty of 3 October 382 by the terms of which Theodosius I settled the Visigoths as Federates not, as formerly, outside the Roman frontier, but inside it in the province of Lower Moesia. For the first time in Roman history an entire barbarian people were given land inside the Empire and were allowed to live there under their own leaders and to observe their own customs. The Roman

[1] Amm. Marc., xxxi. 3. 4 ff.

[2] On the date of the crossing of the Danube see Seeck, *Untergang*, v. 466. On the battle of Adrianople see W. Judeich, 'Die Schlacht bei Adrianopel', *Deutsche Zeitschrift für Geschichtswissenschaft*, vi (1891), 5, n. 1 (site); Thompson, *EG*, 116 f., (method of warfare). Of the course of events in 378–82 Norman H. Baynes, *Cambridge Medieval History*, i. 236, writes that it 'is for us a lost chapter in the history of East Rome. Some few disconnected fragments can, it is true, be recovered, but their setting is too often conjectural. Many have been the attempts to unravel the confused tangle of incidents which Zosimus offers in the place of an ordered history, but however the ingenuity of critics may amaze us, it rarely convinces'. For one such attempt see G. Kaufmann, 'Kritische Untersuchungen zu dem Kriege Theodosius des Grossen mit den Gothen 378–82', *Forschungen zur deutschen Geschichte*, xii (1872), 411–38.

government agreed to pay them annual subsidies, and in return the Visigoths undertook to defend the lower Danubian frontier. This treaty remained in force until 395, when the Visigoths under the leadership of Alaric set out on their fateful journey to the West.

Presumably not every Visigoth left Gothia north of the Danube in 376, just as not every Vandal left Pannonia when the Huns attacked them there in the opening years of the fifth century.[1] But if some Visigoths remained behind in their old homes, they are never heard of again. True, Walafrid Strabo, abbot of the monastery of Reichenau in Austria in 842, says that it was reliably reported in his day that the divine service was still conducted in a Germanic language near Tomi (Constanţa on the Black Sea coast) and elsewhere in the neighbourhood and that copies of the Gothic Bible still circulated there. But if the people whom he had heard of were Goths at all, they are likely to have been Ostrogoths.[2] Yet even when the Visigoths were long gone, their land continued to be called *Gothia*—Orosius (i. 2. 53) calls it by that name as late as 417—presumably because the shifting population and obscurity of conditions there in the tumultuous years which followed the arrival of the Huns on the Danube did not make it easy to attach any more accurate name to the country.

In the lifetime of Ulfila, then, four major wars were fought between his countrymen and the Romans. We can infer a great Visigothic victory in the 340's; but in 332, 367-9, and in 376 and the following years the

---

[1] Procopius, *BV*, iii. 22. 3 ff., with L. Schmidt, *Geschichte der Wandalen*,[2] (Munich, 1942), 13; C. Courtois, *Les Vandales et l'Afrique* (Paris, 1955), 39 n. 5.
[2] Walafrid Strabo, *De eccles. rerum exord. et increm.* vii (Migne, *PL* cxiv. 927); R. Loewe, *Die Reste der Germanen am Schwarzen Meere* (1896), 253; L. Schmidt, 'Weniger bekannte Zeugnisse zur Geschichte der Germanen in orientalischen Chroniken', *Beiträge*, xlviii (1924), 109-13, at 109 f.

Romans inflicted devastating losses on the barbarians, losses which were due more perhaps to hunger than to the sword. Valens' campaigns in 367–9 caused deep and lasting resentment among the Visigoths.[1] The wars of Constantine and of Valens' generals, which were far more disastrous to the barbarians, must have caused an even more profound bitterness. We shall hardly be wrong if we suppose that Ulfila lived his life against a background of deep hostility on the part of his fellow-Visigoths against the Roman Empire. Accordingly, we shall not believe those who suggest that the Visigoths were converted to Christianity because of their 'admiration' for the civilization of the Romans.[2]

[1] See p. 100 n. 1 below. For 376–7 see Thompson, *EG.* 142 f.
[2] For a study of Visigothic history in the years 378–475 see *Historia*, xii (1963), 105–26.

CHAPTER TWO

MATERIAL CULTURE AND SOCIAL ORGANIZATION

No extant writer of antiquity gives us a systematic description of Visigothic society on the eve of the Hun attack in 376. We have no Caesar and no Tacitus to help us here. Our narrative can never consist of a few broad strokes supplemented by an occasional detail. It must be made up of a number of random and isolated details which all too rarely admit of generalization.

1. Material Culture

The Ostrogoths in the Ukraine were unquestionably farmers who supported themselves primarily by crop-raising. It is true that they or their leading men must have mounted themselves on horseback and must have assimilated much of the military technique of the steppe nomads before winning an empire which stretched from the Don to at least the Pripet Marshes and perhaps to the Baltic shores. It is no accident that the only Gothic cavalry which is known to have taken part in the battle of Adrianople is the Ostrogothic cavalry of Alatheus and Saphrax.[1] 'There was a time', said Theodoric Strabo in 478, 'when each Ostrogoth had two or three horses, but now they have no horses and walk through Thrace like infantrymen, just as if they were slaves.'[2] But if their leaders had mounted themselves in the fourth century or earlier, the Ostrogoths as a whole had

---

[1] Amm. Marc., xxxi. 12. 17.
[2] Malchus of Philadelphia, frag. 15 (404. 26 ff., ed. Dindorf).

not altered the basis of their economy. They did not abandon their agriculture and try to support themselves exclusively by their flocks and herds, as they saw the nomads do, whom they had conquered: that would probably have meant a drastic fall in their standard of living. Ammianus describes them, not as nomadic pastoralists, but as living in widely scattered and prosperous villages in southern Russia; and another historian contrasts their agricultural economy with that of the pastoral Huns, who had no interest in agriculture.[1] Unhappily, nothing is known of the Ostrogoths' agricultural methods in the fourth century, but it is difficult to believe that they then had at their disposal the rich variety of agricultural and other implements made of metal which we know that they could make and use in the sixth century when they had long since established themselves inside the Roman Empire: the move into the Imperial provinces undoubtedly brought with it a substantial improvement in the barbarians' implements of production.[2] Late in the fifth century, when our sources for their history become more abundant than they are for the fourth, their economy is still predominantly one of crop-raising though they have herds of cattle, too.[3] This, indeed, was the fundamental weakness of their empire in the Ukraine. The vast areas of those endless plains could only be exploited for a considerable time by mounted nomads, like the Cimmerians and the Scythians and the

---

[1] Amm. Marc., xxxi. 3. 1; Priscus of Panium, frag. 39.
[2] See the description of a late-sixth-century Gothic fort in northern Bulgaria by I. Welkov, 'Eine Gotenfestung bei Sadowetz (Nordbulgarien)', *Germania*, xix (1935), 149–58, with the implements (nearly all of them made of iron) illustrated on 155.
[3] Priscus, loc. cit. (348. 8 ff., ed. Dindorf); Malchus, frag. 16 (405. 19), 18 (416. 20 ff.); cattle, Jordanes, *Get.* liii. 273.

Sarmatians, who had built great empires there in earlier days. But the bulk of the Ostrogoths were sedentary farmers, and when the Huns attacked them c. 370 they paid the price.

Unfortunately, it is impossible to define the difference between the economies of the Ostrogoths and the Visigoths in the middle of the fourth century—if indeed there was any substantial difference at that date. There was certainly a very marked difference between the centralized monarchy of the Ostrogoths, who held down a number of subject peoples, and the social organization of the Visigoths, which we shall study later on. But what can be discovered of the economy of the fourth-century Visigoths? If the Ostrogoths living on the steppe were not primarily pastoralists, it is highly unlikely that the Visigoths living in Dacia were. Scattered throughout contemporary Greco-Roman books there are a number of phrases which would not have been used if in the opinion of the writers the Visigoths had not lived essentially by growing crops. The part of the Visigothic economy which caught the attention of contemporaries was their crop-raising, not their herding: for these are phrases which ancient authors would certainly not have used of the Huns or the Turks and which Tacitus does not use of the Germans of his day.[1] In many passages of fourth-century authors, the Visigoths are spoken of unequivocally as ploughmen, and oddly enough there is scarcely a single reference to

---

[1] *Paneg. Lat.* ii (xii). 22. 3; SHA, *Claud.* ix. 4; Libanius, *Or.* xii. 84; Themistius, *Or.* xvi. 211 B, 212 B, xxxiv. 22; Amm. Marc., xxxi. 3. 8, 4. 5 and 8; Claudian, *vi cons. Hon.* 183 f. (cf. for the Ostrogoths settled within the Empire, idem, *In Eutrop.* ii. 194–7), etc. In contrast to all this, only one author, Sozomen, vi. 37. 4, ascribes an interest in agriculture to the Huns. One author may make a slip of this kind, but it is impossible to believe that six would do so, some of them repeatedly.

them as herdsmen or even as owning flocks and herds (which they certainly did own).[1] We may conclude, then, that the Visigoths were not basically pastoralists, and it may well be that herding was of less consequence to them than it had been to the Germans of whom Tacitus speaks.

If we grant that the Visigoths lived for the most part by tilling their fields, by agriculture, our narrative is nonetheless crippled by the impossibility of defining what exactly we mean by their 'agriculture'. In the present state of the evidence we can say nothing of their agricultural implements or methods (apart from the guess that their implements were less effective and less numerous than they were to become when they had entered the Imperial provinces); and whether or not their agriculture was in any sense migratory and whether the arable was reallocated every year, as had been the German practice in the days of Caesar and Tacitus, are questions which we cannot begin to answer.[2]

A minority of Visigoths will have won a livelihood by other means than agriculture and herding. There was a village, for example, or a hamlet called

[1] SHA, *Claud.* ix. 6; Claudian, *In Rufin.* ii. 126. Their methods of making war confirm that the Visigoths were not a nation of cavalrymen: Thompson, *EG*, 116 f.

[2] The fact that the Visigoths imported grain (p. 38 f. below) does not prove that there had been any 'Rückgang ihrer Kultur' (O. Seeck, *Untergang*, v. 86). The material culture of the Visigoths is briefly discussed by C. Patsch, 'Beiträge zur Völkerkunde von Südosteuropa', *Sitzungsber. d. Akad. d. Wissensch. in Wien: phil.-hist. Klasse*, ccviii, ii (1928), 46 f., but he does not make allowance for the fact that the distribution of wealth among them was unequal, the optimates taking a disproportionately large share. Moreover, he concludes that Bessarabia and Moldavia were more advanced than the rest of Gothia, because the Huns took rich booty there in 376 (Amm. Marc., xxxi. 3. 8) whereas Valens took very little when he invaded Wallachia in 367. But the Huns' onslaught was entirely unforeseen, whereas the Visigoths had plenty of warning of Valens' attack (ibid., xxvii. 5. 2) and were able to evacuate their families and goods to the mountains and marshes before he arrived.

Haliscus, which is described as a harbour.[1] Its site has not been identified, but it was doubtless a tiny port on the Black Sea coast a short distance north of the Danube mouths at which an occasional Roman ship would touch in. The inhabitants of Haliscus probably lived partly by trade, mainly by fishing. Other Visigoths practised the several handicrafts which were highly developed in their society. The vocabulary of Ulfila's Bible includes names for carpenters, smiths, fishermen, potters, doctors, and so on. Most of the potters used the wheel (p. 34 below), and in this there is a clear advance over the conditions of the Germans of the first century A.D. Although their metal-workers appear to have enjoyed a somewhat inflated reputation in modern times,[2] yet the treasure found at Pietroassa (a village near the eastern foot of Mount Istriţa in the county of Buzău some 20 kilometres west-south-west of the town of Buzău)—if it is Visigothic at all—shows that they had attained an exceedingly high degree of skill. Their custom of setting precious or semi-precious stones in their gold-work was an innovation of far-reaching influence in Germanic art at that time and for long after, and it implies not only a high technique and much imaginative power but also a considerable trade in such stones, which seem to have reached Gothia from as far afield as Syria and Persia.[3] Moreover, some

---

[1] Delehaye, 216. 14.
[2] E. Thurlow Leeds, 'Visigoth or Vandal?', *Archaeologia*, xciv (1951), 195–212.
[3] The very widely held view (still maintained by G. Vernadsky, *The Origins of Russia* (Oxford, 1959), 65; M. Mayrhofer, *ZfdA*, lxxxix (1959), 289 f., etc.) that two Goths travelled as far as India in search of precious stones or for some other reason, a view based on an inscription first published by J. Burgess and Bhagwanlal Indragi, *Inscriptions from the Cave-Temples of Western India* (Bombay, 1881), 43 no. 5, 55 no. 33, and frequently re-published, e.g. by Sten Konow, 'Goths in Ancient India',

pieces in the Pietroassa treasure display so curious a mixture of Germanic with Greek and Iranian styles as to show that the craftsmen had learned with extreme skill and initiative from the ancient cultures which surrounded them in Gothia. The objects found at Pietroassa were not all made in the one workshop or at the one time: the Visigothic craftsmen practised this skill in several parts of their country over several generations, and the frequent use at religious shrines of such works of art as those found at Pietroassa must have given steady employment to generations of craftsmen.[1] But before drawing these or other conclusions firmly we must wait until the treasure has been subjected to further study.

Finally, some Goths lived not in Gothia at all but across the Danube in the Roman Empire, where they either enlisted in the Imperial armies or lived as civilians in the cities. One of them, it seems, was a certain Aurgais, who earned enough money and acquired enough Roman culture to set up a charming epitaph over his Roman wife's body when she died in the town of Capidava.[2] Other inscriptions reveal east Germans

Journal of the Royal Asiatic Society (1912), 378–85, Fiebiger, 24 no. 32, should be disregarded in view of W. W. Tarn, *The Greeks in Bactria and India* (Cambridge, 1938), 257 n. 2 (and the whole passage).

[1] A. Odobesco, *Le Trésor de Pétrossa: étude sur l'orfèvrerie antique* (Paris, 1889–1900), iii. 8 ff.

[2] Fiebiger, op. cit., 24 no. 33, 'tunc vixi bene vixi sine nulla crimina vixi resta viator. Acrilla Trygitiani vixit convirginio ann xii et moritur ann xxxv et demisit natos iii. Aurgais posuit memoria coniugi sue. resta viator lege titolo'. This seems to date from the second half of the third century: G. Florescu, 'Fouilles archéologiques de Capidava', *Dacia*, v–vi (1935–6), 351–86, at 381 f.; S. Gutenbrunner, 'Ein germanischer Name aus Capidava', *ZfdA*, lxxv (1938), 115–7; idem, *Germania*, xxii (1938), 54 f. That Aurgais was a German is denied by I. I. Russu, 'Un pretins Visigot in Capidava Dobrogeana', *Revista Istorică Română*, xvi (1946), 173–9, but I am not convinced by his suggestion that *Aurgais* is in fact *Aur(elius) Gai(u)s*.

serving in the armies of the Balkan provinces,[1] and yet others, dating from the late fourth or the early fifth centuries, disclose persons whose names seem to suggest that they were Goths as living in Africa, Gaul, and Italy.[2]

In addition to iron the Visigoths also possessed that other prerequisite of civilization, an alphabet. In 1858 an iron spearhead 15·5 cm. long by 3 cm. broad at its widest part was found some twenty miles from Kovel in Volhynia in the Ukraine. The word *tilarids* (or the like) was inscribed in runes from right to left in silver inlaid in the iron. The inscription has been taken to prove that the Goths were using a runic alphabet in the first half of the third century, if not earlier.[3] But the inscription is presumably Ostrogothic, and there is only one specifically Visigothic rune.[4] This is the brief and hotly debated inscription on a gold ring found among the Pietroassa treasure. (Although we still require proof that the

[1] One is named Busila: H. Vetters, *Dacia Ripensis* (Vienna, 1950), 14 f. Another is Tzita: O. Fiebiger and L. Schmidt, *Inschriftensammlung zur Geschichte der Ostgermanen*, no. 171. For an east German spearhead of the third century found near Vratsa in north-western Bulgaria see K. Tackenberg, 'Germanische Funde in Bulgarien', *Bulletin de l'Institut archéologique bulgare*, v (1928–9), 263–72, at 268 f.; Vetters, op. cit., 16.

[2] Fiebiger-Schmidt, op. cit., nos. 170, 173, 175–6, 280. On nos. 172 and 174 see respectively C. Hülsen, *Berliner philologische Wochenschrift*, xxxix (1919), 124, and A. Riese, *Germania*, iii (1919), 64, who point out that these inscriptions have nothing to do with the Goths.

[3] H. Arntz and H. Zeiss, *Die einheimischen Runendenkmäler des Festlandes* (Leipzig, 1939), 19–41, with bibliography, to which add W. Krause, 'Der Speer von Kowel, ein wiedergefundenes Runendenkmal', *Germanien* N.F., iii (1941), 450–64. But G. Must, 'The Inscription on the Spearhead of Kovel', *Language*, xxxi (1955), 493–8, suggests that the inscription is neither runic nor Germanic, but Illyrican; and J. W. Marchand, 'Les Gots ont-ils vraiment connu l'écriture runique?', *Mélanges F. Mossé* (Paris, 1959), denies that the Goths knew the runes at all.

[4] For other alleged 'runes' which have been found in Rumania and which are none of them genuine runic inscriptions see K. Horedt, 'Funde der Völkerwanderungszeit aus Siebenbürgen', *Anuarul Institutului de Studii Classice*, iv (1941–4), 163–79, at 168 ff.

objects of which the treasure was composed are Visigothic, there seems little reason to doubt that the runic inscription was carved by a Visigothic hand.) There is no reason to believe that by the middle of the fourth century more than a handful of Visigoths were literate. It would be easy to exaggerate the use which they made of writing even after Ulfila had invented his alphabet (an achievement which was remembered and admired even by Catholics writing long after he was dead).[1] On the other hand, the fact that runes were used very extensively among the Scandinavians in the fifth and sixth centuries suggests that in the fourth century the Goths, who influenced Scandinavia so profoundly and who were so far in advance of it, were making a much more widespread use of writing for magical or religious purposes than the solitary surviving inscription might at first sight indicate.[2]

It is difficult to resist the impression that in their material civilization the Visigoths had advanced considerably beyond the level reached by the Germans of whom Tacitus speaks. It is true that we cannot answer many of the fundamental questions which arise concerning their society. We may guess, in view of what is known about St. Saba (p. 53 below), that land was no longer owned by the kindreds and that some Visigoths

---

[1] Apart from Philostorgius, ii. 5 (who was not a Catholic), see Socrates, iv. 33. 6; Sozomen, vi. 37. 11; Jordanes, *Get.* li. 267; Eugenius of Toledo, *carm.* xxxix. 6, xl *fin.*; cf. E. Wölfflin, 'Joca Monachorum', *Monatsberichte d. kön. preussischen Akad. d. Wissensch. zu Berlin* (1872), 106–18, who cites (p. 118) from a seventh-century uncial MS. of Schlettstadt: 'qui primus litteras Gutigas invenit? Goulphyla Gotorum episcopus'.

[2] For the Pietroassa rune see esp. Arntz and Zeiss, op. cit., 52–97, 443, with a bibliography to which add W. Krogmann, 'Der Runenring von Pietroassa', *Wörter und Sachen*, xxi (1940–1), 26–52; H. J. Graf, *Germanisch-romanische Monatsschrift*, xxxi (1943), 128 f.; S. Gutenbrunner, *Zeitschrift für deutsche Philologie*, lxxxiii (1964), 257–66.

had been dispossessed of their land altogether. Little can be deduced at present about the quantities of iron which were at their disposal. Their weapons, in so far as they were made of metal at all, were of iron, and their arrows were tipped with it.[1] Although there is no evidence that the Dacian gold-mines were exploited in the fourth century,[2] it would indeed be surprising if Visigothic stocks of iron were no greater than those of the Germans in general 300 years earlier. Roman money will have been no less widely used as a means of exchange in the interior of Gothia than it had been in the interior of Tacitus' Germany. We have seen that there appear to have been islands of sub-Roman civilization in Gothia far from the frontier; and the inhabitants of these old Roman cities probably introduced the Visigoths to the use of money as a means of exchange. Moreover, Roman merchants were no less likely to bring Roman coins into southern Gothia than they had been to bring them into the frontier regions of first-century Germany. Indeed, there was one feature of Visigothic life which was wholly alien to the Germans of Tacitus' day: Roman-Gothic trade was fundamental to the very existence of Visigothic society in the form which that society had taken on by the middle of the fourth century, and if the Roman government closed the frontier to traders the effect on the Visigoths was disastrous.[3] But there are two matters which seem decisive. Unlike the Germans of Tacitus' day, the Visigoths were making almost universal use of the potter's wheel (p. 34 n. 1 below), a fact which in itself suggests that they had larger centres of population than

[1] Amm. Marc., xxxi. 7. 14.
[2] O. Davies, *Roman Mines in Europe* (Oxford, 1935), 205 f.
[3] See p. 19 f. above.

had been known in the first century. And the clearest evidence of all is the fact that writing began in Ulfila's day to play a decisive part in Visigothic life, for it was used not merely to preserve magical formulae but also to propagate ideas. This alone is sufficient to indicate a much higher degree of complexity and advancement in fourth-century Visigothic society than anything that had been known in Germany in the time of Tacitus.

2. Trade with the Roman Empire

A Visigothic graveyard of the fourth century was excavated in 1903 at Sântana de Mures (formerly Marosszentanna) on the right bank of the river Mures some three kilometres north-east of Târgu Mures (formerly Marosvásárhely). Most of the seventy-four graves, in so far as they had not been robbed, were well furnished with pottery and small ornaments and the like. There were on the average four or five pots to each grave, though one child's grave contained as many as twelve and some contained none at all. Some of the pots are of Roman manufacture, some closely resemble Roman pots, others are identical with the Ostrogothic pottery of the Kievan area. Of over one hundred pots scarcely a dozen had not been turned on the wheel.[1] Not a single weapon was found during the excavations, although a two-edged sword was discovered before systematic digging began. (This absence of weapons

[1] Of the seven pots found at Aldeni only one appears to be handmade: G. Ştefan, 'Une tombe de l'époque des migrations à Aldeni (Dép. de Buzău)', *Dacia*, vii–viii (1941), 217–21, cf. Figure 1 (no. 5). All three of the pots found at Lechinţa de Mures were wheelmade: Beninger, art. cit. (on p. 3 n. 3 above), 123 f. Handmade pottery was not owned by the poor only: see Kovacs in the first of the articles cited on p. 35 n. 3 below, tomb no. 40, which includes a handmade pot, though the tomb is obviously that of a well-to-do woman who owned several silver ornaments.

from their graves is characteristic of the Visigoths, though not of the contemporary Vandals and Burgundians, throughout their history.)[1] A number of small iron knives, some of which were found in women's and children's graves, could not be classed as weapons. The buckles, brooches, and rings were mostly made of bronze, seldom of iron, sometimes of silver. There were several silver pendants. There were bone combs, needles, spindles. There were considerable quantities of cornelian and of blue and green and yellow glass beads, skilfully cut into several facets and showing in their style strong Roman influence. There were round beads of amber and of black paste with white inlay, and the like. Glass was otherwise represented by a single conical cup of Roman manufacture.[2] Besides the pottery there were also found the bones of pigs, sheep, and poultry in some of the graves. Cremation was unknown: the body was laid fully clothed in a trench, and the earth was heaped over it.[3]

These finds are relevant to our purpose in two ways. First, one of the most striking features of them is that in several respects they are practically indistinguishable from the contents of some of the Ostrogothic graves

[1] The absence of Visigothic weapons in Rumanian excavations cannot be taken as proof that the Visigoths lived on peaceful terms with the Romano-Dacians whom they found in their country: contra, G. I. Brătianu, 'Le problème de la continuité Daco-roumaine', *Revue historique du sud-est européen*, xx (1943), 46–70, at 60.

[2] For a similar conical glass beaker of the third or fourth century which is thought to have been found at Apulum see Horedt, art. cit. (on p. 6 no. 2 above), 165.

[3] On these excavations see I. Kovacs, *Dolgozatok: travaux de la section numismatique et archéologique du musée national de Transylvanie à Kolozsvar*, iii (1912), 250–367, of which I have read only the very full French summary; cf. Brenner, art. cit. (on p. 8 n. 3 above), 262–7. The excavations at Târgu Mureş yielded objects very similar to those found at Sântana: see Kovacs's further article in *Dolgozatok*, vi (1915), 226–325. (Kolozsvar is now Cluj.)

from the neighbourhood of Kiev; and it seems that in spite of the very different circumstances in which the two peoples were living many of the material objects of Visigothic society had undergone little change as a result of their settling in Dacia.[1] In the second place, the finds show that both Ostrogothic and Visigothic art and life had been subjected to considerable influence by Roman craftsmen and traders. Roman trade with the Ostrogoths was well developed, and many a trader must have gone up the Bug and the Dnieper and tramped or rode mile by mile from one Ostrogothic village to another. As for the Visigoths, not only had Roman traders access to the sub-Roman population of the countryside (p. 7 above) and towns of Gothia, but Roman pottery and glass found their way to the Visigoths themselves deep in Gothia.

On the other hand, there is a piece of evidence which suggests that Visigothic tastes had exercised some influence on the Roman inhabitants of Transdanubian Dacia before Aurelian's evacuation of the province. In a Roman grave found in Bruiu (Braller) in the Kökel valley there was discovered a silver brooch of the third century which shows clear traces of Pontic-German influence. The tomb dates from the Roman period of the occupation of Dacia or perhaps from shortly after the official Roman withdrawal, but it is in any case the grave of a Roman.[2] Indeed, the possibility cannot be

[1] I know the Ostrogothic finds only from P. Reinecke, 'Aus der russischen archäologischen Litteratur', *Mainzer Zeitschrift*, i (1906), 42–50; M. Ebert, 'Ausgrabungen bei dem "Gorodok Nikolajewka" am Dniepr', *Prähistorische Zeitschrift*, v (1913), 80–100, 110–3; L. Kilian, 'Gotische Irdenware aus dem Gebiet und Museum Berditschew', *Alt-Preussen*, viii (1943), 8–10.
[2] K. Horedt, 'Völkerwanderungszeitliche Funde aus Siebenbürgen', *Germania*, xxv (1941), 121–6, at 121; idem, 'Frühgeschichtliche Funde aus Siebenbürgen', *Deutsche Forschung im Südosten*, i (1942), 33–42, at 35 f.

excluded that some of the 'Visigothic' objects found in Gothia may in fact have been made or at any rate owned and used by the Romano-Dacian inhabitants of the country. Moreover, a number of characteristically Gothic bronze brooches—fibulae 'with returned foot'—have been found in what is now Bulgaria. One has been discovered in a Germanic context near Madara (some fifteen kilometres east of Kolarovgrad), another in the neighbourhood of Kolarovgrad (formerly Shumen), a third not far from Stara Zagora. They date from the third and fourth centuries, and it is not necessary to believe that all of them were dropped by Gothic raiders. Gothic civilians and Gothic troops serving in the Imperial forces could often enough be seen south of the Danube (p. 30 f. above); and the local Roman inhabitants may have made some of these brooches on Gothic models or may have acquired them by way of trade with Gothia.[1]

Trading across the frontier brought much profit not only to the Visigoths but also to Roman merchants in the various frontier cities as well as to the ubiquitous Syrian traders who came into Gothia.[2] It is said, for example, that Maximinus, who afterwards became Emperor, retired from the army in the reign of Macrinus (217–8), bought land and settled down in the Thracian village where he had been born, and then carried on trade continuously with the Goths beyond the frontier.[3] Our authority is unreliable, and objections can readily be raised to some points in his story;

---

[1] Tackenberg, art. cit. (on p. 31 n. 1 above), 264–6.
[2] Schulze, op. cit. (on p. 2 n. 2 above), 529 n. 3. For Syrians in Transdanubian Dacia in an earlier period see *CIL* iii. 7761, 7915. They were active on the west coast of the Black Sea in the sixth century also: V. Beshevliev, 'Altchristliche Grabinschriften aus Varna', *Bulletin de la société historique bulgare*, xix–xx (1944), 18–39.
[3] SHA, *Maxim.* iv. 4.

but there seems little reason to doubt his implication that in the fourth century, when he was writing, landowners in the Balkan provinces sometimes had an interest in the Transdanubian trade. It may be that not all the Roman merchants who went into Gothia before 376 were petty, independent pedlars each working on his own account. Some of them may have been the agents of large Roman landowners trading the products of Roman villas for the slaves and raw materials of the Goths. In the view of the Imperial government in 369, however, the Visigoths had used their trading facilities to inflict damage on the provincials whose cities they were allowed to enter. Hence the restrictions which Valens imposed on them after his victory in 369 (p. 14 f. above). This was a severe blow to a people whose need for Roman imports was as pressing as that of the Visigoths; and the fact that they accepted this restriction of their trade, according to a contemporary Roman, was an indication that they had surrendered unconditionally in 369.[1]

The character of the goods exported by the Romans is partly revealed by the nature of the subsidies which the Visigoths, in return for leaving the Imperial provinces in peace, had received from the Roman government with some intervals since the middle of the third century. The subsidies were very substantial, and in the opinion of one Roman they were more costly to the Empire than the raids which they were designed to prevent. They took the form of coin, grain, ship-loads of clothing, and other unspecified articles.[2] This

[1] Themistius, Or. x. 135 D τοῦτο δὲ ἦν ἅμα μὲν σημεῖον τοῦ πάντα ἐπιτάττοντα τοῖς βαρβάροις τὰς σπονδὰς ποιεῖσθαι (x. Valens).

[2] Ibid. 135B; cf. Julian, Caes. 329 A; Eusebius, Vit. Const. iv. 5. The subsidies are attested in the reign of Alexander Severus: Peter the Patrician, frag. 8; Zosimus, i. 24. 2; Zonaras, xii. 21; cf. Jordanes, Get. xvi. 89.

suggests that the goods imported from the Roman market towns also included grain (which was certainly exported at this time to the pastoral nomads of south-eastern Europe),[1] and cloth, to which may be added a number of luxury goods, like some of the objects excavated at Sântana de Mures—pottery, glass, combs, and doubtless other articles, such as wine, which have not survived.

Their trade with the Empire influenced the language of the Visigoths in a striking degree. Roman traders together with the hundreds of Visigoths who returned home from service with the Imperial forces planted an interesting list of Latin words in the Gothic language before the middle of the fourth century and before Ulfila took up his pen. Greek influence on Gothic was almost exclusively ecclesiastical, but the Latin words which established themselves in Gothic—and well over a score are known—have an exclusively military and commercial character.[2]

What did the Visigoths export in return for their imports? We have already seen that large numbers of fourth-century coins have been found in Visigothic territory. Many of them doubtless belonged to the submerged Roman population of the country—indeed, a fourth-century hoard of coins was found at Orşova (county of Severin) along with other Roman objects in the ruins of a Roman house.[3] Doubtless, too, many of them arrived in Gothia by way of the subsidies paid

---

[1] Themistius, *Or.* xxx. 350 A, which is interesting in that it illustrates the dependence of the nomads on imports from the settled agricultural populations with whom they came in contact.
[2] M. H. Jellinek, *Geschichte der gotischen Sprache* (Berlin and Leipzig, 1926), 179 ff.; Schulze, op. cit., 511 n. 2; E. Schwarz, *Goten, Nordgermanen, Angelsachsen* (Berne and Munich, 1951), 35 ff., etc.
[3] Macrea, art. cit. (on p. 3 n. 2 above), 303.

over by the Roman government and the pay brought back by individual Visigothic soldiers who had enlisted in the Roman army.[1] Yet it can scarcely be questioned that a high percentage of these coins must have reached the Visigoths as a result of their trade with the Empire. That would explain why many of them lie on the trade routes which ran from the Danube northwards to the great passes over the Transylvanian Alps.[2] Since the Visigoths, then, possessed so many Roman coins, we may conjecture that they sometimes paid for Roman imports in Roman coins: the subsidies may not have been entirely lost to the Empire.

But the chief export of the Visigoths was slaves. When the Emperor Julian was preparing in 362 for his great campaign against the Persians, some of his advisers urged him instead to attack the Visigoths. Julian replied that he was looking for worthier foes, for the Goths were not a match for the Galatian dealers by whom they were offered for sale everywhere, high and low alike.[3] Indeed, a law passed by the Imperial government about a dozen years after Julian had spoken these words suggests that slaves were the most important commodity imported by Roman traders from the barbarian world in general.[4] Not the least enthusiastic among the slavers were the officers commanding the garrisons on the Danube, and their purchases and sales of slaves reached high proportions

---

[1] Eusebius, *Vit. Const.* ix. 7; Libanius, *Or.* lix. 92; Amm. Marc., xx. 8. 1 (cf. xxiii. 2. 7); Zosimus, iii. 25. 6, and p. 31 n. 1 above.

[2] Jung, art. cit. (on p. 6 n. 2 above), 13 f.; C. Schuchhardt, 'Wälle und Chausseen im südlichen und östlichen Dacien', *Archäologisch-epigraphische Mittheilungen aus Oesterreich-Ungarn*, ix (1885), 202–32, at 230.

[3] Amm. Marc., xxii. 7. 8.

[4] *Cod. Justin.* iv. 63. 2 (?374): why otherwise are *mancipia* specified in that law?

about the year 370.[1] They were still hoping to procure domestic slaves, agricultural workers, and herdsmen as well as concubines and fancy boys from among the Visigoths who crossed the river in 376.[2] But even before that date the number of such slaves scattered over Thrace alone was very high, and a writer of Julian's own time or earlier seems to suggest that there was scarcely a region of the Empire which did not possess its Gothic slaves. And these slaves were not less numerous at the end of the century, when years of warfare had delivered many a Visigoth into the hands of the Romans.[3]

That the Galatian dealers were able to organize manhunts in Visigothic territory without the permission of the Visigothic leaders is scarcely credible. They may indeed have done so occasionally, but for the most part they will have simply bought the slaves from free Visigoths; and if so, the implication would seem to be that some Visigoths would enslave members of their own people (though not perhaps members of their own tribe or of their own clan) and would sell them to the Roman merchants. That is why the many slaves from Gothia who could be found in the Thracian provinces in and before 376 were actually Visigoths: they are not said to have been Vandals or Gepids or Sarmatians whom the Visigoths had captured in their numerous border forays and had then sold to the Galatian dealers. True, many a prisoner taken in these wars must have

---

[1] Themistius, *Or.* x. 136 B φρουράρχας δὲ καὶ ταξιάρχας ἐμπόρους μᾶλλον καὶ τῶν ἀνδραπόδων καπήλους, οἷς τοῦτο μόνον ἔργον προσέκειτο πλεῖστα μὲν ὠνήσασθαι, πλεῖστα δὲ καὶ ἀπεμπολῆσαι.

[2] Eunapius, frag. 42 (239. 4, ed. Dindorf); Zosimus, iv. 20. 6.

[3] Amm. Marc., xxxi. 6. 5 'ex eadem gente multitudo, dudum a mercatoribus venundati'; SHA, *Claud.* ix. 5 'nec ulla fuit regio quae Gothum servum triumphali quodam servitio non haberet'; Synesius, *de Regno*, 23 D.

ended his days in slavery to the Visigoths or the Romans, but the slaves to whom Julian referred were neither Sarmatians nor Gepids: they were Visigoths by birth. Although not all the Romans who were taken prisoner by the Visigoths were necessarily reduced to the condition of slaves,[1] yet some of the more well-to-do Visigoths themselves possessed slaves of their own and were able to take them across the Danube in 376.[2] Unfortunately, there is no information about the nationality of these slaves of the Visigothic optimates, and whether they, too, were Visigoths is not clear. But doubtless it would have been difficult to keep many Visigoths enslaved in Gothia itself, and these slaves may well have been Vandals, Gepids, Sarmatians, or Romans. There is no valid evidence for inter-tribal warfare among the Visigoths before 376 (pp. 87 ff. below), a fact which also suggests that slaves in Gothia were not usually Visigoths. But there is no evidence to show how those who were sold to the Romans had been reduced to bondage in the first place. They may have been enslaved through failure to repay loans (though to assume the existence of debt-slavery at this date is perhaps somewhat hazardous) or they may have been sold by husbands or parents who could not otherwise save them from starvation.

The evidence of archaeology, of the vocabulary of the Gothic language, and of the literary authorities all combine to show that trade between Gothia and the Roman provinces was very highly developed; and when the archaeology of Rumania has been thoroughly explored it may well be found that Roman imports

[1] See E. A. Thompson *apud* M. I. Finley (ed.), *Slavery in Classical Antiquity* (Cambridge, 1960), 197 f.
[2] Amm. Marc., xxxi. 6. 5; Eunapius, frag. 42 (239. 17 and 20, ed. Dindorf); Jordanes, *Get.* xxvi. 135; cf. SHA, *Claud.* vi. 6.

were as numerous there in the fourth century as they
had been in Bohemia in the first century.

3. Social Organization

The contemporary historian Eunapius speaks more
than once of the tribes (*phylai*=no doubt *pagi*) of the
Visigoths,[1] and these tribes sometimes associated
together in a confederacy in order to achieve specific
military aims. In 364 the help sent by the Visigoths to
the usurping Emperor Procopius was despatched not
by one confederate leader but by a number of chiefs,
presumably tribal chiefs, independently.[2] Again, raids
were carried out at many points along the Danube at
this time (p. 17 above), and the phrases which our
authorities use to describe them suggest that they were
the work of clan or tribal levies or of retinues.[3] But soon
after 364 the tribes associated together in a confederacy,
and Athanaric then makes his first appearance in
history: he is the confederate leader.[4] This confedera-

[1] Frag. 55 (248. 22 and 26), 60 (251. 31). I do not discuss the evidence
of Tacitus, *Germ.* xliii. 6, on the Goths, for it relates to a time 250 years
earlier than that under discussion, and it may in fact be inaccurate.

[2] Amm. Marc., xxvi. 10. 3. There is no trace of a confederate leader
in Libanius, *Or.* lix. 89 (A.D. 348–9), who speaks of their leaders in the
plural; and yet there was a Judge in 347–8: Auxentius, 75. 21.

[3] Themistius, *Or.* x. 136 C; Amm. Marc., xxvi. 4. 5; but note Zosimus,
iv. 10. 1; cf. Seeck, *Untergang*, v. 88.

[4] Amm. Marc., xxvi. 6. 11. That Athanaric obtained his position as
confederate leader only on the eve of the war of 367–9 was shown by
T. Hodgkin, *Italy and Her Invaders*, i, i (Oxford, 1892), 161 n. 1. The
first fairly certain reference to him is, I think, Eunapius, frag. 37 (233. 27;
234. 13), cf. Zosimus, iv. 7. 2, referring to 366. Isidore, *Hist. Goth.* 6 (ii.
269), says that Athanaric was king for 13 years (cf. the *Laterculus* of the
Visigothic kings in *Chronica Minora*, iii. 464). Since his command
terminated towards the end of 376, this figure (if we count inclusively)
suggests 364 as the year of his election; and it is precisely in 364 that
Ammianus describes the Visigothic nation as 'conspirantem in unum'.
The tribes united and the confederate leader was chosen in that year. It
is improbable, then, that Athanaric was the 'sacriligious Judge' who
expelled Ulfila *c.* 347.

tion of the tribes was maintained in existence for many years owing to the exceptional circumstances of the times—the war against Valens in 367–9, the attack of the Huns in 376, the flight from Gothia to the Roman provinces, and the subsequent struggle with the Romans. But when a temporary security returned at last to the people in 382—the year in which they settled as Federates in Moesia—we seem to hear no longer of a confederate chief but once more of a plurality of leaders.[1] The confederation of the tribes was no longer necessary in the new conditions of peace and comparative security, and so it was dissolved and the tribes resumed their independent life until for reasons which are unknown the confederacy was revived once more for a time in the period 383–92 (p. 159 below). In the fourth century, then, the confederation was a temporary and recurring arrangement and did not exist continuously.

The terms used by Roman writers to denote Visigothic military leaders fall into two classes. The first class consists largely of diminutives, *regalis, regulus, archon, basiliskos*.[2] It is unlikely that those chiefs who are referred to by diminutive names were military leaders of the entire people; and in fact several of them could hold their 'office' at one and the same time. In a period for which information is particularly full Winguric, Atharid, and the unnamed 'leader' (*archon*) of the *Passion of St. Saba* were in existence at the same time as the Judge Athanaric. This term 'Judge' forms the second class of name given to Visigothic leaders. It is found in four entirely independent authors; and it is

---

[1] Themistius, *Or.* xvi. 210 B (A.D. 383), τοὺς ἐξάρχους καὶ κορυφαίους, though this, of course, is scarcely conclusive.

[2] *Passio S. Sabae*, 219. 3; Anon. Vales., 27; Jordanes, *Get.* xxvi. 135; and for the *archon* Winguric see p. 159 below.

clear that *iudex, dikastes*, 'judge', was a semi-technical or even an official name among the Romans for a certain type of Visigothic leader. Further, the Judge was a chief with powers superior to those of other chiefs.[1] Granting that the society as a whole was a tribal one, the interpretation of these facts is clear. The Judge is the confederate leader and only appears at a time when the tribes have associated in a confederacy, whereas the minor, subordinate chiefs are tribal leaders, the chiefs of *pagi*, whose existence is explicitly vouched for by Eunapius (though the Germanic *pagi* are not said to have been headed by chiefs in Tacitus' day).[2] There is no indication in any of our sources that there was a confederate leader in normal times of peace, and there is no reason to think that in the middle of the fourth century the Judge had to be chosen from any 'royal clan'. Indeed, there is ample evidence for the existence among the Visigoths of that dual leadership which is often attested among other Germanic peoples but which is never found where there was a 'royal clan'.[3]

The name 'Judge' which the Romans gave to the confederate chief suggests that he had judicial functions of some kind (though there is no evidence that in

[1] Amm. Marc., xxvii. 5. 6 and 9, xxxi. 3. 4; Ambrose, *de Spiritu Sancto* prol. 17 (Migne, *PL* xvi. 736) *iudex regum*; Auxentius, 75. 21; Themistius, *Or.* x. 134 D (who in *Or.* xi. 146 B, xv. 190 D more loosely refers to Athanaric as *dynastes*). There were also *iudices* among the Quadi: Amm. Marc., xvii. 12. 21.

[2] Eunapius, frag. 60 *init.*

[3] See Jordanes, *Get.* xvi. 91, xxi. 112 (cf. SHA, *Gord.* xxxi. 1 *Argunt*); Amm. Marc., xxxi. 4. 8, cf. 5. 5; Sueridus and Colias, ibid., 6. 1, and see p. 159 below. Athanaric had no colleague, but when Isidore, *Hist. Goth.* 6 (ii. 269), says that 'Athanaric was the first of the Visigoths to undertake the administration of the people', we may wonder whether or not he means that Athanaric was the first confederate leader to be appointed without a colleague. The fact that Geberic (p. 54 below) had no known colleague means little, as our sources for his period are so defective. On the 'royal clans' of the other Germans see Thompson, *EG*, 34 f.

Tacitus' day the military leader ever acted as judge); but our authorities do not specify what these judicial functions may have been. Whether he had any religious duties is also obscure. During the persecution of the Christians in 369–72 Athanaric instructed some unspecified persons—and they may have been priests— to place a cult object (*xoanon*) on a wagon, wheel it round to each tent where a Christian was known to live, and order these Christians to worship the object and make sacrifice.[1] So the Judge may have had influence, at any rate in some matters, over the priests, though there is no reason, of course, to suppose that his office was essentially a priestly one. His major functions, however, in so far as they have been recorded, were neither judicial nor religious but military, for it was usually warfare that brought his office into being. In wartime he was the leader of the Visigothic forces. But the degree of centralization which a tribal society can achieve must not be exaggerated. When Athanaric led the resistance to the Huns in 376 he did not do so at the head of all the Visigothic warriors: a number of the clans took no part in the struggle and merely gave way to panic when they heard of Athanaric's defeat.[2] Again, the Judge's personal powers seem to have been little if at all greater than those of Arminius among the Cherusci in the early first century A.D. When the Romans referred to Athanaric as *basileus*, 'king', he considered it important to repudiate the title and requested that he should be called 'Judge' instead, 'for the former term implied authority, but the latter wisdom'. The distinction was of importance to him and

[1] Sozomen, vi. 37. 13.
[2] Amm. Marc., xxxi. 3. 8. Cf. the lack of cooperation with the rest of the Visigoths on the part of Sueridus and Colias and their men: ibid., 6. 1.

was still of importance to the historian Jordanes, himself a Goth, nearly two centuries later; for he speaks of their 'headmen and leaders (*primates et duces*) who commanded them instead of kings (*reges*)'.[1] Accordingly, when the Judge wished to initiate any major change of policy or of strategy he proceeded by 'persuading' and 'urging' his followers, like Arminius long ago, and not by simply issuing direct orders to them.[2] Even after the Visigoths had entered the Roman Empire in 376 the chieftainship does not appear to have grown much stronger. Alaric would seem to have had little more power in this respect than Fritigern had had. He 'consults' with his council and 'recommends' plans, but he does not impose them, for the confederate council still retains its rights. The poet Claudian paints a vivid picture of Alaric consulting with and receiving criticism from his council; and the poet shows how fierce was the criticism of a leader by his people when his leadership became unpopular.[3] Athanaric did not negotiate alone with Valens in 369 but was accompanied by some of the leading men.[4] The decision to enter Roman territory in 376 was only taken after prolonged deliberation by the majority of the people: it was not a personal decision on the part of Fritigern.[5] Such consultations could be stormy and were sometimes the scene of sharp divisions

---

[1] Themistius, *Or*. x. 134 D; Jordanes, *Get*. xxvi. 134; cf. Tacitus, *Ann*. ii. 44. 3, 'Maroboduum regis nomen invisum apud populares ... habebat'. The distinction between the *duces* and the *rex* of the Lombards is made by Paulus Diaconus, *HL* i. 14; and for the Franks see Greg. Tur., *HF* ii. 9 *init.*, and *Chron. Min.* i. 301, s.a. 451, 'non enim tunc reges gens Francorum habebat sed ducibus contenti erant'.

[2] Amm. Marc., xxxi. 6. 4, cf. 12. 9, *mollire, allicere*; Jordanes, *Get*. xxv. 131.

[3] Claudian, *BG* 479 ff., *vi cons. Hon*. 242 ff.; cf. Sidonius, *Carm*. vii. 452 f.; Jordanes, *Get*. xxix. 147.

[4] Amm. Marc., xxvii. 5. 9; Themistius, *Or*. x. 132 D.

[5] Amm. Marc., xxxi. 3. 8; cf. Jordanes, *Get*. xxv. 131 *communi placito*.

of opinion, as they had been in the days of Arminius.[1] In fact, there seems to have been just as little individual authority in fourth-century Gothia as there had been in Germany in the first century.

Sometimes our Roman authorities regard the nobility as the decisive factor in wartime even when they were nominally serving under a confederate chief.[2] As for times of peace, the persecution of the Christians in Gothia in 369–72 was initiated by the confederate council while the tribal chiefs were merely responsible for seeing that the persecution was actually enforced (p. 71 below). When the council decided to persecute the Christians the tribal leaders went round the villages to see how the council's instructions were being carried out; and when a chief as representative of the council came to a village the members of the village council would appear before him and would give him the information which he required. But the tribal and confederate chiefs were simply the instruments through which the confederate council acted. In times of peace and indeed for the most part in wartime also even the confederate chief is not known to have had any power over the life, liberty, and property of the tribesmen except in so far as he carried out the decisions of the council. What control did the council exercise over the chief? That the chiefs were elected in the period under discussion cannot be doubted, for more than one reference is made to the election of chiefs in the years 376–418, and a growth of popular rights in the interval may be ruled out as impossible.[3] And that the electoral body consisted of the council of the optimates rather

---

[1] Amm. Marc., xxxi. 16. 1.   [2] Ibid., 7. 7–9, 15. 13.
[3] Orosius, vii. 43. 10; Jordanes, *Get.* xxx. 158, xxxiii. 174; Isidore, *Hist. Goth.* 20 (ii. 276).

than of the assembled warriors will seem probable in a moment. We do not know whether the council also possessed the power to depose a chief. When Athanaric failed in his defensive operations against the Huns in 376 and was no longer able to secure a sufficient supply of food for his people, the people 'deserted' him; and they reappear under the leadership of Fritigern and others, none of whom is regarded as a rebel or usurper.[1] Perhaps the term 'deposition' implies a more formal act than was in practice customary or necessary.

Who composed the confederate council is not clear. Eunapius describes its members as men who were 'outstanding in rank and birth', and they may well have been the chiefs of the tribes, whom he also mentions.[2] They were easily distinguishable from the humbler Visigoths by the more costly clothing which they wore and by their slaves; indeed, in 376 they were able to bribe the Roman commanders on the Danube by offering them quantities of linen and of tasselled rugs.[3] Archaeological finds show that the more well-to-do warriors among the Germanic peoples living to the west of the Visigoths possessed valuable and beautifully ornamented articles of personal adornment, weapons, and so forth; and there can be little doubt that further archaeological research in Rumania will show something of the richness and beauty of the personal possessions of the Visigothic optimates, too.[4]

What of the third great organ of government of which Tacitus spoke, the general assembly of the warriors? In

---

[1] Amm. Marc., xxxi. 3. 8 f.   [2] Frag. 60 init..
[3] Idem, frag. 42 (239. 2 f., and 18). Slaves: ibid.; Amm. Marc., xxxi. 6. 5; Jordanes, Get. xxvi. 135; cf. SHA, Claud. vi. 6.
[4] Note the golden shoe-buckle inset with garnets which is now preserved at Brasov: E. Beninger, Der westgotisch-alanische Zug nach Mitteleuropa (Leipzig, 1931), 32 f., with Figure 8.

49

St. Saba's village, and so no doubt in all the villages of Gothia, there were meetings attended by the villagers at which affairs of common interest were discussed.[1] But there is no evidence that the gathering of Saba's fellow-villagers could have discussed a matter which was not of purely local interest, a matter of policy affecting Gothia as a whole. It is improbable, for example, that before the persecution of the Christians began the question of whether it should be instituted at all was discussed at countless village assemblies up and down Gothia. In other words, the assembly at Saba's village was a very different thing from, and was no substitute for, the kind of assembly of the warriors of which Tacitus spoke. There is in fact no evidence to show that a general assembly of the warriors existed at all among the fourth-century Visigoths; and it can be taken as virtually certain—for our evidence for early Visigothic society is by no means negligible—that such an assembly did not exist.[2] There may have been religious festivals or ceremonies held at longer or shorter intervals at which the majority of the warriors would assemble and so would have an opportunity of discussing affairs of common interest. Such seem to have existed in Tacitus' day,[3] and the eleventh-century Swedes held a great festival every nine years at which the people would come together and no doubt could discuss whatever they wished to discuss, though in an

[1] These village councils may have existed in some form until a very late date, though perhaps with different functions: *Legg. Visig.* viii. 5. 6, 'in conventu publico vicinorum'.

[2] None of the passages cited by C. Sanchez-Albornoz, 'El aula regia y las asambleas politicas de los Godos', *Cuadernos de Historia de España*, v (1946), 5–110, at 6–13, proves the existence of a general assembly. The *Vita Aviti* to which he refers is the *Vita S. Aviti in Petracoricis*, for which see *Acta Sanctorum*, iv June 292–4: it is worthless as a source for the reign of Alaric II.

[3] *Germ.* xxxix. 2.

unorganized way.[1] But if similar assemblies existed among the Visigoths our authorities say nothing of them. Again, when the whole host of the people went out to war the warriors could deliberate on questions of general importance; and in 376 'the greater part of the people' after lengthy deliberations decided to abandon Gothia and the war against the Huns and to enter the Roman provinces (p. 47 n. 5 above). When Theodoric I was killed at the battle of the Catalaunian Plains in 451 the assembled Visigothic warriors proclaimed his son Thorismud as king.[2] But such cases are a very different thing from the holding of regular meetings at which the bulk of the tribesmen could have the final say on all important matters of internal and external policy. This absence of the general assembly of the warriors is perhaps the most striking difference between the society of the Visigoths in Athanaric's time and the society of the Germans as a whole described by Tacitus. Although general assemblies of the villagers existed in the various villages for settling local affairs (p. 66 f. below), popular control of the business of Gothia as a whole had been removed.[3] The optimates can now be said to wield political power, though they have not yet got control of a State machinery which would make their power absolute.

In Tacitus' day the leading men had been acquiring power by means of their retinues. The evidence for the part played by this institution among the Visigoths before 376 is defective. In the early years of the kingdom

[1] Adam of Bremen, iv. 27, though cf. H. M. Chadwick, *The Origin of the English Nation* (Cambridge, 1907), 298.
[2] Jordanes, *Get.* xli. 215.
[3] It is not impossible, of course, that elected representatives of the rank and file took part in the deliberations of the optimates, as at the council of the Old Saxons in the eighth century: see Thompson, *EG*, 42 n. 1. There is no hint in our sources to support such a theory.

51

of Toulouse (after 418) the retinue was an institution
recognized by Visigothic law; and it had not come into
existence in the first place as a result of the settlement
in southern Gaul.[1] Our authorities refer to the retinues
of Athanaric, of Fritigern and Alavivus, and of Alaric,
whose 'companions' are carefully distinguished from
his kindred.[2] Athanaric's 'companions' deserted him
after 378, for he had remained at peace, it seems, during
the glorious campaigns of 377–80 so that his followers
had no share in the renown and booty won by those
who had followed Fritigern across the Danube; and
Alaric, too, is said to have feared that failure would lead
to his desertion by his retinue. In this respect at any
rate the retinue was still what it had been in the first
century: the 'companions' remained with their leader
only so long as he could ensure a steady intake of
plunder and fame. The leader also gave arms and other
gifts to his followers, just as he had done in Tacitus'
day.[3] Again, when the tribal chief Atharid was helping
to enforce the persecution of the Christians in Gothia he
came to a village with 'a company of lawless brigands'
who referred to Atharid as their 'master' (*despotes*) and
who included one of his sons among their number.[4] It is
difficult to see what can have been the relationship of
these men with their 'master' if it was not that of a
retinue with its leader; for the men were not slaves, and
who else had a master in Gothia? If this phalanx was in

[1] *Cod. Euric.* 310, 311; *Legg. Visig.* v. 3. 1.
[2] Athanaric: Amm. Marc., xxvii. 5. 10, xxxi. 4. 13; Socrates, v. 10. 4;
cf. L. Schmidt, *Geschichte der deutschen Stämme: die Ostgermanen* (Munich,
1934), 418 n. 2. Fritigern: Amm. Marc., xxxi. 5. 6; Jordanes, *Get.* xxvi.
136. Alaric: Claudian, *vi cons. Hon.* 314 f. There is a long and not very
fruitful discussion of the Visigothic *comitatus* in C. Sanchez-Albornoz, *En
Torno a los origines del Feudalismo* (Mendoza, 1942), i. 19–39.
[3] *Cod. Euric.*, loc. cit. That the *buccellarii* were *comites* was shown by E.
Oldenburg, *Die Kriegsverfassung der Westgoten* (Diss. Berlin, 1909), 29 f.
[4] *Passio S. Sabae*, 219. 3, 220. 2 and 6.

fact Atharid's retinue, it is of the utmost interest to observe that it was used not in a plundering raid against another people but so as to enforce 'order' at home and to coerce a refractory tribesman.[1]

Whatever may have been the form and the function of the retinue among the Visigoths at this date, the decay of their tribal system is not a matter of speculation. Quantities of property had begun to accumulate in private hands before 376, and political power was also tending to concentrate in private hands. This is strikingly illustrated in a vivid scene which is described in the *Passion of St. Saba*. When an unnamed tribal chief in the course of the persecution of 369–72 came to Saba's village and heard that the Saint was an unrepentant Christian, he turned to the members of the village council, who were present, and asked them whether Saba owned any property. He was told that Saba owned nothing more than the clothes on his back. Thereupon the chief considered the Saint to be of no importance and said 'Such a man can neither help nor harm us', and ordered him to be driven from the village forthwith.[2] Clearly, at that date not only had private property associated itself in the chief's mind with social power but the poor man, unlike the man of property, could 'neither help nor harm' the execution of the confederate council's resolutions. Sharp divisions of wealth had put an end to the general equality of the tribesmen.

Another indication of the growth of private wealth and of the consequent decay of the old social system is the tendency for the chieftainship to become hereditary

---

[1] Ibid., 220. 31 ff., though the men's inclination to set Saba free and so to disobey Atharid's order to kill him does not reinforce our feeling that they may have been his retinue.

[2] *Passio S. Sabae*, 218. 11 ff.

and to descend from father to son, as it is not known to have done in the days of Tacitus. There is no valid evidence that a 'royal clan' existed among the Visigoths before Alaric's time,[1] but Atharid was 'the son of the kinglet (*basiliskos*) Rothesteus'. The unnamed father of the Judge Athanaric was so powerful and important that Constantine had seen fit to appease him by erecting a statue of him in Constantinople: he was surely a Judge like his son after him.[2] Again, the 'queen' Gaatha was the widow of a Judge; and when she wished to enter Roman territory she left the 'kingdom' (*basileia*) or the 'power' (*exousia*) to her son Arimerius as a legacy; and her action is in no way described as illegitimate.[3] Now, lack of evidence makes it difficult to compare these examples of hereditary chieftainship with the practice of the Visigoths in earlier times. But there is some reason for thinking that it was an innovation, for in spite of their fame and heroism the father and the ancestors of Geberic (an early-fourth-century Visigothic chief) were not the leaders of the Visigoths as a whole: his predecessors in office were Ariaric and Aoric, who are not said to have been in any way related to him.[4] But if the confederate and tribal chieftainships sometimes descended from father to son later in the fourth century, that by no means implies that the son succeeded by any legal right and without election. Even in the latest days of the Visigothic kingdom of Spain hereditary succession to the throne never established itself.

[1] Nothing can be built on Zosimus, iv. 25. 2, 34. 3: see E. A. Thompson, *Attila and the Huns* (Oxford, 1948), 10. On the Balthi see P. Grierson, 'Election and Inheritance in Early Germanic Kingship', *Cambridge Historical Journal*, vii (1941), 1–22, at 11 f.

[2] *Passio S. Sabae*, 219. 3; Themistius, *Or.* xv. 191 A. Note the importance attached to the chief's son in Anon. Vales., xxxi; *Passio S. Sabae*, 220. 6.

[3] Delehaye, 279. For parallels to her action see Grierson, art. cit. 8 f.

[4] Jordanes, *Get.* xxi. 112 ff., cf. xxxi. 162.

Moreover, the confederate council was able to exert stronger pressure on the villages than the latter, we may suspect, would have submitted to in the days of Tacitus. Village affairs in the fourth century were discussed, as we shall see, by a council of village elders or leading men and were then submitted to a general assembly of the villagers for approval or discussion (p. 66 below). But we know of a case where the confederate council's decision was resisted by the villagers, or, at any rate, the villagers did without enthusiasm what they were ordered to do. In any case, their resistance or reluctance was fruitless.

It seems, then, that a central authority consisting of the optimates, meeting in the confederate council, could dictate policy, at any rate in some matters, to the Visigoths at large; and there was no general assembly of the warriors to keep the optimates in check. Popular control of society had declined markedly as compared with the conditions described by Tacitus, and this can hardly be dissociated from the sharp differences of wealth which had now made their appearance in Gothia. An optimate is prepared to say openly and brutally that the opinion of a poor man carries no weight. But the optimates still lacked regular machinery for imposing their will on society as a whole. It was easy enough to coerce a single individual like Saba; but how could they coerce a substantial number of warriors? Severe internal struggles took place between 376 and 418 before the old social organization could be wholly thrown off and a new one established in its place which gave the optimates coercive machinery.

4. Paganism

We have practically no detailed information about the religious beliefs and practices of the pagan Visi-

55

goths.[1] It is true that their very name 'Visigoths' preserves something of their superstition (according to philologists), for while the term *Ostrogothi* means 'East Goths', the name *Visigothi* or *Vesegothae* does not mean 'West Goths', which would, we are told, be some such form as **Wistrogoti*. But like several other Germanic peoples (though unlike the Westphalians and the men of Wessex) they shrank from calling themselves by the name of the ill-omened West, where the sun sinks and dies away. And so they took the similarly-sounding but better-omened name of *Visi* or *Vesi* (*Visigothi* does not appear until the fifth century) which means the 'valiant' or 'gallant' people; and their fear of the ill-omened West can be traced far into the fifth century.[2] But on the whole their subjective emotions and attitudes towards the gods, towards natural phenomena, and towards the outside world in general are very obscure. Of the evil spirits and demons, the spirits of the wood-land, magic rites relating to the dead, and so on, we can say little more than that they existed or were thought to exist.[3]

Their religion was organized on a tribal basis when

---

[1] On Gothic paganism see esp. K. Helm, *Altgermanische Religionsgeschichte* (Heidelberg, 1937), ii. 1.

[2] H. Wehrle, 'Die deutschen Namen der Himmelsrichtungen und Winde', *Zeitschrift für deutsche Wortforschung*, viii (1906–7), 333–52, at 334–7; P. Kretschmer, 'Austria und Neustria', *Glotta*, xxvi (1938), 207–40, esp. 231 ff.

[3] Helm. op. cit., 22 ff. Apart from the evidence discussed here other details about Visigothic religion and religious practice could no doubt be elicited from the linguistic evidence (though Helm's work shows how little certainty the unsupported linguistic evidence has so far given) and even from archaeology. Thus, the inscribed ring found at Pietroassa is often thought to have been an oath-ring, on which see F. P. Magoun, 'On the Old-Germanic Altar- or Oath Ring', *Acta Philologica Scandinavica*, xx (1949), 277–93. For another example, the word *hraiwadubo*, see Helm, op. cit., 22; H. Vetters, 'Der Vogel auf der Stange—ein Kultzeichen', *Jahreshefte des österreichischen archäologischen Instituts in Wien*, xxxvii (1948), 131–50, some of whose arguments seem hazardous.

they crossed the Danube in 376. Each tribe which
entered Roman territory possessed rites and ceremonies
common to all its members. Each tribe carried across
the river the sacred cult objects connected with these
rites and was accompanied by the tribal priests and
priestesses.[1] The tribal religion was carefully mono-
polized by the tribesmen and was not discussed with
persons who were not members of the tribe. At any rate,
Eunapius twice emphasizes the 'profound and adamantine silence' which the Visigoths maintained about their
rites and cult objects in conversation with the Romans.[2]
But it may be that the contents of a sacred treasury have
been found in the astonishing hoard of twenty-two gold
objects discovered in 1837 at the Rumanian village of
Pietroassa (p. 29 above). This treasure is commonly
believed to have been buried amid the confusion of the
Hun attack in 376.[3] It was composed exclusively of gold
vases, cups, and ornaments of a sacerdotal nature, and
it contained no weapons, no household utensils, and no
women's jewelry; and we need have little hesitation in
believing that these immensely valuable objects belonged to a sanctuary.[4] It would be of great interest to

[1] Eunapius, frag. 55. The priests are also mentioned by Ambrose, *Ep.*
x. 9, on which see R. Egger, 'Die Zerstörung Pettaus durch die Goten',
ibid., xviii (1915), Beiblatt 253–66. For parallels to the priestesses see J.
de Vries, *Altgermanische Religionsgeschichte* (Berlin and Leipzig, 1937), 263;
cf. Chadwick, op. cit., 317 ff., etc. Priestesses are not known to have
existed at all among the contemporary West Germans.
[2] Eunapius, frag. 55 (248. 28, 249. 13).
[3] Odobesco, op. cit. (on p. 30 n. 1 above), iii. 15 ff.
[4] The runic inscription on the armband, which is usually (though by
no means always) transliterated as 'gutan iowi hailag', cannot be interpreted as meaning 'Sacred to the Jove of the Goths', as was first proposed
by R. Loewe, 'Der Goldring von Pietroassa', *Indogermanische Forschungen*,
xxvi (1909), 203–8: see R. Meissner, 'Die Inschrift des Bukarester
Ringes', *ZfdA*, lxvi (1929), 54–60, 213–6; de Vries, op. cit., ii. 94;
Arntz and Zeis, op. cit. (on p. 31 n. 3 above), 79 ff., though the old
interpretation is still given by T. Karsten, 'Die Inschrift des Goldrings
von Pietroassa', *Beiträge zur Runenkunde und nordischen Sprachwissenschaft = G.*

know whether this treasure was associated with a cult which was common to the Visigoths as a whole or whether the treasure was the possession of a tribe (*pagus*). If the former, nothing is known of this common cult or of the priests and ceremonies attached to it. No one priest, so far as is known, had the status among the Visigoths which the *sinistus* held in Burgundian society late in the fourth century; for the authority of the *sinistus* was superior to that of all other Burgundian priests and he was not liable to deposition, unlike their military leaders.[1] On the other hand, no priest is recorded to have played any part in the procedure which led up to the martyrdom of St. Saba, of which we have a detailed description; and if a village priest had been at all prominent in bringing the Saint to his doom, the author of the *Passion of St. Saba* would scarcely have missed the opportunity of drawing attention to him. Among the Visigoths, then, we hear only of tribal priests and priestesses, never of a clan or village priest and never of a priest of the people as a whole.[2] In this the Visigothic priesthood differs not only from that of the Burgundians but also from that of the Germanic peoples of whom Tacitus speaks, for the

Neckel Festschrift (Leipzig, 1938), 78–82. The precise meaning of *hailag* is disputed. It is not used by Ulfila, who perhaps avoided it in his translation of the Bible because its associations were too closely involved with pagan belief. But taken in conjunction with the nature of the objects of which the treasure was composed, the word certainly suggests the cult character of the treasure. With the armbands and necklaces of Pietroassa, cf. Ambrose, loc. cit.

[1] Amm. Marc., xxviii. 5. 14; cf. the *sacerdos civitatis* of Tacitus, *Germ.* x. 2 and 4, the *primus pontificum* of the Northumbrians in Bede, *HE* ii. 13, and the *princeps sacerdotum* of the South Saxons in Eddius, *Vita S. Wilfrithi*, xiii.

[2] Ulfila has to devise the word *ufargudja* to translate ἀρχιερεύς, though admittedly if the Visigoths had a special name for a pagan high priest Ulfila might not have cared to use it in his translation of the Bible: see G. W. S. Friedrichsen, *The Gothic Version of the Gospels* (Oxford, 1926), 169 ff.

functions of the priests in the first century A.D. seem to have been almost confined to public ceremonies affecting the whole people: they took omens on public occasions, they had duties in connexion with the meetings of the assembly of the warriors, and they had the guardianship of the sacred groves and of the holy emblems which were kept in them. But they do not appear to have taken any part in any ceremony affecting a smaller unit of society than the people as a whole.[1] Whatever may have been the practice in the case of private sacrifice among the Visigoths, the essential point is that their priests were tribal priests and that there is no evidence for the existence of a high-priest of the whole people. Hence, it may not be too hazardous to assume that the treasure of Pietroassa, if it is Visigothic at all, was a tribal possession.

Of the character of Visigothic tribal worship we know that it included something like ancestor-worship, a common feature in tribal societies, for it both expresses and sanctions the authority exercised by the tribal leaders. According to Jordanes, the Visigoths regarded their past leaders not as mere men but as demi-gods, that is, *Anses*, because it was by these men's fortune that they had been led to victory; and Ammianus pictures the Visigothic warriors as they went into battle 'shouting the praises of their ancestors'.[2] The name of the Anses is to be identified with that of the Scandin-

---

[1] H. M. Chadwick, 'The Ancient Teutonic Priesthood', *Folk-Lore*, xi (1900), 268–300, at 270 ff.
[2] Jordanes, *Get.* xiii. 78 (cf. v. 43, vi. 48—even though Thanausis was no Goth); Amm. Marc., xxxi. 7. 11; cf. Claudian, *BG* 528 'di Getici . . . manesque parentum'. The etymology of *Anses* has not been determined: on it see A. Krappe, 'Anses', *Beiträge*, lvi (1932), 1–10, with bibliography, to which add E. Polomé, 'L'Etymologie du terme germanique *ansuz*, "Dieu souverain",' *Études germaniques*, viii (1953), 36–44, with further bibliography in the footnotes.

avian gods called *Aesir*, known from a much later period. In the interval since Jordanes' day, by a process common in primitive religion, ancestor-spirits have grown into outright gods. Unfortunately, we do not know what form was taken by the cult of the Anses. The worship of the dead leader may have been confined to the members of the tribe which he had led in his lifetime or it may have been unrestricted and open to all Visigoths.[1]

In the fourth century they worshipped gods as well as Anses. They worshipped, for instance, a god whom our Latin-speaking authorities call *Mars*.[2] They vowed to Mars as their war-god the first fruits of their booty, they hung spoils on tree trunks in his honour, and the sacrifices offered to him may even in the fourth century have included human victims, prisoners of war.[3] Now, it can scarcely be doubted that these gods were common to all the Visigoths: they were not tribal gods, but the worship of them may well have been organized on a tribal basis. Nothing that is known of either the Anses or the gods gives us reason to doubt Eunapius' statement that Visigothic religion was essentially a tribal affair. Moreover, during the persecution of the Christians in

[1] The comparative evidence does not help us to decide this question: see G. Landtman, *The Origin of the Inequality of the Social Classes* (London, 1938), 125 ff.

[2] Jordanes, *Get.* v. 41. Note, too, the reference of the Arian bishop Maximinus to the 'Mars qui aput Tracias natus ibi est defunctus', *JTS*, xvii (1916), 327. (On the attribution of that work to Maximinus see p. 120 below). These are the only references in ancient literature to a specific Visigothic deity.

[3] Jordanes, loc. cit. See de Vries, op. cit., i. 251 f. Over fifty passages relating to human sacrifice have been collected from all over the Germanic world by E. Mogk, *Abhandlungen d. kön. sächsischen Gesellschaft d. Wissensch.: phil.-hist. Klasse*, lxxxi, 17 (1909), 601–43. Jordanes seems to imply that the custom had been abandoned by the time the Goths settled on the shores of the Black Sea, but in view of Radagaisus' sacrifice in 406 this implication may not be wholly correct.

Gothia in 369–72 Athanaric ordered a *xoanon*[1] to be placed on a cart and wheeled round to the dwellings of persons suspected of being Christians, who were ordered to worship it and make sacrifice. No doubt the purpose of wheeling the *xoanon* about was normally to fructify the fields and animal life.[2] It is difficult to believe that the emblem was anything other than a tribal one. For if it had been unique and had been regarded as the holy possession of the entire people Athanaric would have been confronted with the task of wheeling it about from one end of Bessarabia to the other end of Transylvania, an improbable procedure whether it was drawn by the men themselves or by a lumbering team of cattle. In other words, our authority is dealing with a local incident of the persecution and is referring to the *xoanon* of the particular tribe to which those Christians belonged who were subsequently martyred: other tribes will have had other *xoana*. And if it is agreed that the *xoanon* was tribal, then the men

[1] This may have been a wooden post like the Saxon Irminsul of a later time; cf. the somewhat similar Germanic gods in Ibn Fadlan's account of the northmen, translated by A. S. Cook, 'Ibn Fadlan's Account of Scandinavian Merchants on the Volga in 922', *Journal of English and Germanic Philology*, xxii (1923), 58, and the much disputed figures in A. Banduri, *Imperium Orientale* (Venice, 1729), ii. 417, Figure ix, conveniently reproduced in H. Bradley, *The Goths* (London, 1891), 14. Banduri's figures, alleged to be reproduced from the Column of Arcadius, are ascribed mysteriously and apparently without reason to Gentile Bellini, who was in Constantinople in 1479: E. Müntz, 'La colonne théodosienne à Constantinople', *Revue des études grecques*, i (1888), 318–25. There is nothing like them in any of the more trustworthy descriptions of Arcadius' Column, e.g. in E. H. Freshfield, 'Notes on a Vellum Album, etc.', *Archaeologia*, lxxii (1922), 87–104. On the other hand, it is known that although these pictures are unreliable they are not wholly without some basis in reality: J. Kollwitz, *Oströmische Plastik der theodosianischen Zeitalter* (Berlin, 1941), 21 f., so that it would be desirable to know more about their origin before rejecting their authority outright.

[2] Sozomen, vi. 37. 13. Cf. the parallels in Tacitus, *Germ.* xl, and in the *Indiculus Superstitionum et Paganiarum*, xxviii, 'de simulacro quod per campos portant'; de Vries, op. cit., i. 182 f.; Chadwick, op. cit., 220–51.

who saw to its transportation, if they were priests at all, must have been tribal priests. And so the incident would form another piece of evidence for the tribal priesthood and for the tribal organization of religion which Eunapius explicitly mentions.

The only specific Gothic festival known to us is the Yule festival, which is attested in the surviving fragment of the Gothic Church Calendar, for in it November is called *fruma Jiuleis*, the 'first Yule', the implication being that at least one other Yule followed it. This festival is also attested in month-names and other evidence among the Anglo-Saxons, the Norwegians, and the Icelanders. It was designed to help the seeds to germinate and to bring good crops, and what is of interest to us is that among the northern peoples, and hence perhaps among the Goths, too, it was not a festival celebrated at one central holy place by all the people together, but a local (probably clan or tribal) festival.[1]

The evidence, then, suggests that Visigothic religion was of a type that is in no way surprising in a developed tribal society. The essential point is that such evidence as is forthcoming—and it is obviously very meagre— never contradicts, and sometimes seems to support, the explicit assertion of Eunapius that Visigothic religion was organized on the basis of the tribes (*pagi*); and in fact there is no good evidence for the existence of any common cult or sanctuary or festival in which the whole people took part together. Now, a tribal religion does not proselytize: it has no adherents outside the tribe, and we have mentioned the 'adamantine' silence with which the Visigoths surrounded their cults when they

[1] M. P. Nilsson, *Opuscula Selecta* (Lund, 1951), i. 296–311, esp. 303. See further p. 92 below.

came in contact with the Romans. What would happen, then, to the tribal religion when the tribal organization itself died away and the former tribesman felt that no exceptional bond united him with those who had once been his kin? It seems certain that the tribal organization was destroyed when the Visigoths settled inside the Roman Empire after 376 and that the kindreds and *pagi* then ceased to have any significant existence.

CHAPTER THREE

THE *PASSION OF ST. SABA*
AND VILLAGE LIFE

A complete text of the *Passion of St. Saba* and of certain kindred documents was published by Delehaye more than half a century ago. These works give us priceless information about early Visigothic Christianity and especially, of course, about Saba himself, who was martyred on 12 April 372. They are also invaluable for the study of the society which produced Ulfila and the Gothic Bible. The *Passion* does what the works of Caesar and Tacitus never do—it brings us for the first time into a Germanic village and enables us to see something of how the villagers managed their own affairs. Yet it has received strangely little attention either from students of Roman history or from students of early Germanic society.

The *Passion* is in fact a letter written by the Church in Gothia to the Church in Cappadocia on the occasion of their sending the saint's body to that province: they inform the Church of Cappadocia of the circumstances in which Saba had died.

Saba was a Goth, according to the letter, and a fervent Christian from his childhood, speaking peacefully to all on behalf of the truth. He had no possessions beyond what was necessary for his day-to-day life. When the *megistanes* (as the letter calls the optimates, the tribal nobility) began to move against the Christians, requiring them to eat meat which had been sacrificed to idols, Saba publicly refused to obey their orders. As

64

a result he was expelled from his village, but after a while he was allowed to return home. In a second outburst of persecution the villagers were prepared to swear that there were no Christians in their village, but again Saba foiled them. He would not allow them to swear such an oath: 'Let no one swear on my behalf, for I am a Christian.' Again he was expelled.

Later on a third and 'mighty' persecution broke out. It was just before Easter 372, and Saba wished to go to another village so as to celebrate Easter with the priest Guththica. But he had a vision on the road. A man of tall stature appeared to him and told him to return to the priest Sansalas; but Saba said, 'Sansalas is away'. He had fled to the Roman Empire to escape the persecution, but because of the approach of Easter he had in fact returned home, though Saba did not know this. A heavy fall of snow blocked Saba's road so that he was obliged to go back home, and there he found Sansalas. They celebrated Easter together, but on the third night thereafter Atharid, the son of a chief called Rothesteus, arrived in the village with some of his henchmen, seized the two Christians, bound them, and took them away and tortured them.

When morning came, the persecutors saw that Saba's body was unmarked. They therefore tied his hands and feet to the ends of two cart-axles, and laying him spreadeagled on the ground they tortured him until far into the following night. When they fell asleep a woman who had got up early to prepare food for her household came and set him free; and when morning came and the persecutors awoke, they found the saint busily helping the woman with her work. They tied him up again and suspended him from a beam of the house. After a while there came men from Atharid carrying

65

sacrificial meat and bade Saba eat it. Once more he refused. One of Atharid's sons then tortured him again, but he did not cry out nor did his body show any mark.

Atharid thereupon ordered him to be killed. Leaving Sansalas, who had also been maltreated, Atharid's men took the saint to the river Musaeus (Buzău) in order to drown him. But they were in fact willing to let him go— how could Atharid ever find out, if they released him? —but Saba told them to get on with their business; and so they threw him into the water and held him down with a piece of wood until he drowned. The Roman *dux* of the province of Scythia Minor sent men to recover the body and bring it back; and it was now being sent to Cappadocia.

That is the story in outline as told by the letter to Cappadocia. Let us examine some parts of it in more detail.

At the beginning of the narrative the villagers are required by order of the megistanes to eat sacrificial meat in public. How this decision of the megistanes was conveyed to the villagers is unknown. But village affairs are discussed in the first instance by a village council;[1] and this council has determined that the villagers among them who are Christian must be spared in spite of the order of the megistanes: the Christians in their midst shall merely be induced to eat unconsecrated meat rather than sacrificial meat so that a true test may be avoided and the persecutors cheated. This is the plan on which the council has decided, but it must be discussed by all the villagers assembled

---

[1] The council-members are referred to in the phrases τισὶν ἐθνικοῖς τῶν κατὰ τὴν κώμην, Passion 217. 28, τινὲς τῶν ἐκ τῆς προειρημένης κώμης ἐθνικῶν 218. 4, οἱ κόμητες, 218. 9. The first of these phrases does not denote simply a random group of moderates, for it is explicitly stated that they had the power to expel Saba from the village.

together before it can be put into practice.[1] Saba like the other villagers has the right to speak, and he comes forward on two separate occasions and uses his right boldly: he will not allow any such subterfuge as the village council had suggested—he will never deny his Christianity. Accordingly, the plan put forward by the council members has to be modified; and when a representative of the megistanes comes round to the village to see how the test is progressing, the village councillors tell him that in fact there is one Christian among them—Saba himself.

The whole of this scene described in the third chapter of the *Passion* is a vivid representation of a clan society in action. There is no indication that Saba's procedure in disagreeing with the council's decision was illegitimate or even unusual. He merely expressed freely an opinion which was unpopular or at any rate a nuisance. The scene does not quite prove that the decisions of the villagers had to be unanimous before action could be taken, though this may have been the case. At any rate, there was no machinery for suppressing Saba's opinion or for preventing him from making his views known to the visiting chief; and still less was there any means of compelling him to change his attitude and to fall in with the opinion of the majority. Nor was Saba an isolated case. We learn from another source that in addition to Saba other Christians were given an opportunity of coming forward and speaking bravely on behalf of the faith in their respective villages.[2] A further point is also noteworthy. After his first speech refusing to eat the meat the village council compelled Saba to

[1] 217. 34 τοῖς πᾶσι, 36 τοὺς πάντας, 218. 7 τῷ συνεδρίῳ.
[2] Sozomen, vi. 37. 12, who adds, however, that some were not given the right to speak. But Sozomen is not authoritative when he speaks of the internal life of a barbarian people beyond the Roman frontier.

leave the village for a while, but then they permitted him to come back.[1] Now, this does not in itself mean that the freedom of the villagers was disappearing and that a man who expressed an unpopular opinion was liable to be penalized. Saba, as we shall see, had offended against the gods of the community by refusing to share their meal; and an offence against the gods was an offence against the community itself. Saba's temporary expulsion was due to this offence—his refusal to take part in the sacrificial meal of the villagers—and not to the unpopularity of his opinions as such or to his being a Christian. The fact that he was a Christian was known to the villagers throughout the proceedings and even before the proceedings began, and was not resented by them. Indeed, when the news reached the village that the persecution had been initiated the first thought of the village councillors was how they could save Saba. The temporary expulsion, then, was not due to Saba's Christianity but to his unwillingness even to make a show of joining in the sacrificial meal. To that extent the expulsion was unconnected with the persecution as such.

It is a pity that it was not to the author's purpose to tell us more about the sacrifice and the sacrificial meal, which evidently formed an integral part of Visigothic village life. In a clan society the communal eating and drinking were a symbol and a confirmation of mutual social obligations. The man who refused to eat the sacrificial meat with his fellows thereby dissociated himself from their religion and from their social duties and rights: he had made himself an outcast.[2] That is

[1] 217. 36 ff.
[2] Cf. F. Kauffmann, 'Altdeutsche 'Genossenschaften', *Wörter und Sachen*, ii (1910), 9–42, at 20 ff.; V. Grönbech, *The Culture of the Teutons* (Oxford, 1931), ii. 179, and esp. 182 f.

probably why the public eating of sacrificial meat was regarded by the megistanes as a test for men suspected of having become Christian.[1] On the other hand, it is noteworthy that when he was first expelled from his village Saba was soon allowed to return. On the second occasion the villagers might not have expelled him at all if pressure had not been put upon them by the visiting chief; and even then the saint might well have been spared if the village councillors could have shown to the persecutor that Saba was a man of some property (p. 53 above). But even so Saba was not lynched: action was not taken on the spur of the moment without a hearing of the merits of the case. On the contrary, the case was heard, and the action was taken by a man who had some measure of recognized authority. True, Saba was not put to death by his fellow-villagers: the men who killed him came from outside the village. Yet the villagers in the end did nothing to help him, but abandoned him to his fate. He had put himself outside their protection by his refusal to join in their sacrificial feast. Now, the presbyter Sansalas does not seem to have been a Visigoth, for he is thought to bear an Asian name;[2] and he was presumably descended from the Asian prisoners who had been carried off by the Goths during their great raids on Asia Minor in the mid-third century. Accordingly, it is of great interest to notice that Sansalas was not requested, so far as we know, to

---

[1] *Passion*, 217. 28, 219. 31; Sozomen, vi. 37. 14. Cf. a very revealing passage in *Heimskringla: Hakon the Good*, xviii. There could be no doubt, at any rate in later times, as to where a German Christian was obliged to take his stand on this issue: see Pope Gregory II in the correspondance of Boniface, *Ep.* xxvi (A.D. 726) in *MGH. Epistolae Selectae*, i, ed. M. Tangl (1916), 46.

[2] R. Loewe, 'Der gotische Kalender', *ZfdA*, lix (1922), 245–90, at 277 f.; idem, 'Gotische Namen in hagiographischen Texten', *Beiträge*, xlvii (1923), 407–33, at 431.

partake of the sacrificial meal, and although he was tortured he was not put to death. His crime was less than that of the Visigothic tribesman Saba. Sansalas' offence was that he was a Christian, and this in a man of Asian descent was an offence during the period of the persecution but it was not a capital offence. Saba's crime was that he had offended against the gods of his people, and for this as a Visigoth he became an outcast and was put to death.

To return to the village council: we do not know how this was chosen or who composed it. We might perhaps guess that it consisted of elders who were noted for their long experience of affairs and for their wisdom or for their prowess as warriors or hunters. At any rate, the council's two known functions were, first, that it represented the village in meetings with a member of the confederate council, and, secondly, that it discussed the business of the village before bringing it to the general assembly of the villagers. In this last point it resembles the council which pre-considered the business that was to come before the general assembly of the warriors in the first century A.D. The 'national' council, as it were, which Tacitus describes in his *Germania* (xi. 1) is reproduced on a smaller scale by the village council referred to in the *Passion*. Finally, it may be observed that there is no mention of a village chief or headman, and if one had been present at these proceedings the author of the *Passion* could not well have avoided making some mention of him. The unnamed, persecuting 'leader' (*archon*) of the *Passion*, like Atharid after him, comes to Saba's village from outside and knows little or nothing about the villagers. He must be the leader of some larger unit than the village, and I have little doubt that he was one of the 'tribal' leaders, like those referred to by Eunapius (p. 45 above).

What light does the *Passion* throw on these tribal chiefs, as we have called them? If the confederate chief possessed few coercive powers in wartime (p. 46 above), it is unlikely that the tribal chiefs occupied a stronger position in times of peace. True, it would be easy to conclude from one or two sentences in the *Passion* that the persecution of the Christians in Saba's village was initiated by the 'persecutor' or the 'leader', that is, by an unnamed chieftain.[1] But in fact what the *Passion* shows is that the chiefs were merely responsible for seeing that the persecution was actually enforced. A number of phrases in the *Passion* indicate clearly that the persecution was initiated not by any one ruler or chief but by the confederate council. Indeed, in one passage the author explicitly states that Atharid acted 'on the order of the impious ones'. The plural should be noted. It unquestionably means the confederate council, the megistanes; and that the ultimate responsibility for the persecution lay with the megistanes is shown again and again by the language of the *Passion*.[2] When the confederate council decided to persecute the Christians, the tribal chiefs went round the villages to see how the council's instructions were being carried out; and when a chief, as representative of the council, came to a village the members of the village council would appear before him and would give him the information which he required. This, at any rate, was the procedure in Saba's village, and there seems to be no reason why we should not generalize from it. But the tribal chiefs

---

[1] 218. 5 τῷ διώκτῃ, 10 ὁ ἄρχων..
[2] 219. 2 ἐκ τοῦ τάγματος τῶν ἀσεβῶν, 217. 26 f. πρῶτον μὲν γὰρ ὡς ἤρξαντο οἱ κατὰ τὴν Γοτθίαν μεγιστᾶνες κινεῖσθαι κατὰ τῶν Χριστιανῶν, ἀναγκάζοντες αὐτοὺς ἐσθίειν εἰδωλόθυτα, κτλ., cf. 217. 30 f., 218. 3 and 16.

were merely the instruments through which the council acted. In times of peace and indeed for the most part in wartime also even the confederate chief is not known to have had any power over the life, liberty, or property of the tribesmen except in so far as he carried out the decisions of the council. What we should greatly like to have is some information on the part which the village or at any rate the village councillors were allowed to play in the election of a tribal chief. But of this we know nothing. We cannot say whether the humble villagers had any rights at this date when it came to the choosing of a tribal leader.

However that may be, it is certain that the old egalitarian system which Tacitus had described long ago was disappearing among the fourth-century Visigoths. Quantities of property had begun to accumulate in private hands *c.* 370, and political power was also tending to concentrate in private hands. This is strikingly illustrated in a lively scene in the *Passion* to which we have already referred (p. 53 above). It is the scene where the chief, hearing that Saba owned no property, said 'Such a man can neither help nor harm us', and ordered him to be driven out of the village. The mere fact that the author of the *Passion* turns aside to record this remark of the chief's would seem to suggest that the words were in his opinion significant and disturbing: in connexion with these words he calls the chief *anomos*—he was no respecter of tribal custom. Even at that date, then, private property meant social power, and the poor man was a political cipher.

Moreover, the *Passion* makes it clear that the confederate council, the megistanes, were able to exert stronger pressure on the villages than the latter, we may suspect, would have submitted to in the days of which

Tacitus speaks (p. 55 above). The fact is that to some extent the persecution of the Christians in 369–72 was imposed on the villages from above, and it was the megistanes who specified the test of the public eating of the sacrificial meat without any consultation, so far as we know, with the rank and file of the Visigoths. And worst of all, although the village council in Saba's village did not approve of the persecution, there was, it seems, no means of protesting to the megistanes against it. They do not appear to have had the right to dissociate themselves from it, still less to say bluntly to the megistanes that they would have nothing to do with it. When the megistanes issued an order, the villagers had to give at least the appearance of obeying it. This is an illustration of the meaning of the disappearance of the general assembly of the warriors which we mentioned above (p. 50 above). So the council in Saba's village was reduced to a subterfuge in its effort to avoid carrying out the orders of the megistanes: they proposed to allow Christians to eat unconsecrated meat instead of sacrificial meat 'so that they might keep their own men unharmed, and deceive the persecutors'.[1] In the second wave of persecution the council was actually willing to declare without ado to the persecutor that there was no Christian in their village. They were even prepared to make this declaration on oath, a fact which suggests that enthusiasm in the village for the decisions of the megistanes was slight. But once again the obstinacy of Saba himself foiled their well-intentioned deceit; and they admitted with some reluctance that in fact there was one Christian among them (though in fact there were others besides).[2] Thereupon the chief, who had come to the village to see how the persecution was

[1] 217. 31.   [2] 217. 33 ff.

progressing, 'ordered' Saba to be driven out of the village. On the first occasion on which Saba was expelled it was the village council who had ordered him to go. But on the occasion of the second expulsion the village council appears to have been given no voice in the matter: they simply received instructions from the tribal chief to drive Saba out.[1] In the final wave of persecution the henchmen of Atharid were able to beat and torture Saba without any consultation with the rest of the villagers and without bringing any charge against him, though it may be significant that Saba was taken from the village by night and suffered thus when not actually present in his own village.

What the *Passion* reveals, then, is democracy within the village but nothing that could be called democracy in the relations between the village and the central authority. Political power has to some extent become concentrated in the hands of the optimates, and the village council is no longer in a position to assert its rights boldly on every issue that affects it. But individual Visigoths were not afraid to disobey outright the most stringent orders of the tribal chief who represented the megistanes. We have seen how, when the men guarding Saba fell asleep, an old woman took pity on him and set him free. Had she not been willing to defy the confederate council the saint might well have finished his career then and there. Also noteworthy is the willingness of Atharid's own men to set Saba free in outright defiance of Atharid's orders: the saint had to insist that they should do their duty and carry out their instructions. Finally, the whole course of events in Saba's village shows that feelings for one's neighbour were stronger than respect for the orders of the optimates.

[1] Contrast 218. 1 with 15.

It must be emphasized that all the evidence which we have suggests that the Christians in Gothia in Ulfila's time were in general drawn from the humbler strata of society. The descendants of the Roman prisoners taken in the raids on Asia Minor in the third century will scarcely have been of much social influence among the Visigoths. The Christian priest and his associates who were used by Fritigern as intermediaries during his negotiations with the Emperor Valens in 378 are explicitly said to have been humble persons.[1] The bishop of the Audian sect (p. 83 below) called Silvanus was presumably the descendant of Roman prisoners. True, he may have been a Visigoth who adopted this Roman name on his conversion; but to believe that is merely to multiply hypotheses, and in fact Epiphanius describes him not as a Goth but as being 'from Gothia'.[2] It can scarcely be doubted that Ulfila himself, like Selenas after him, was also the offspring of a very humble, though not servile, family in Gothia, and not being a pure-blooded Visigoth he would not have been a member of any clan. His foreign descent would have rigorously excluded him from membership, unless he had been willing to undergo the pagan rites of initiation and adoption, which in a man of Ulfila's uncompromising Arianism can scarcely be considered as a possibility. It is true that three arguments have been put forward to show that Ulfila was a well-to-do and perhaps even a noble Visigoth; but these arguments cannot stand.[3] They are (i) that he was free to leave Gothia in 348

---

[1] Amm. Marc., xxxi. 12. 8 'Christiani ritus presbyter ... cum aliis humilibus', though he says nothing (15. 6) of the social status of the other Christian whom he mentions as being associated with the Visigoths.

[2] Epiphanius, *Panar. Haeres.* lxx (iii. 247 f., ed. Holl).

[3] They are suggested by H. Giesecke, *Die Ostgermanen und der Arianismus* (Leipzig and Berlin, 1939), 9.

when the first persecution took place; but then it would follow that all those who were driven out or who fled in the persecutions were well-to-do, which can hardly have been the case; (ii) that he acted as ambassador to Constantius; but the Christian who acted as ambassador to Valens, as we have just seen, is known to have been of humble birth—these Christians were doubtless chosen as envoys because as Christians they might carry more weight with the Romans than barbarian pagans could do; (iii) that Eusebius of Nicomedia would not have made him bishop if his position among his people had not been a distinguished one; but Eusebius' action only suggests that Ulfila's position was distinguished not among the Visigoths as a whole but among the Christians in Gothia—and his distinction was due not to his birth or wealth but to his learning. Finally, the one Visigothic Christian about whom detailed information has survived, Saba, is explicitly stated to have owned no property whatever and to have been therefore of no political account.[1] At all events, nothing in our evidence suggests that the tribal nobility had been seriously affected by Christianity in the decades preceding 372; and indeed the *Passion* gives us positive evidence to the contrary, for it was 'the megistanes throughout Gothia' who had decided on the persecution in the first place.[2]

The reasons which induced the megistanes to enforce the persecution will be examined later on (p. 98 below). But it seems certain that the Visigoths at large did not care very much whether one of their number ate the sacrificial meat or not—it would be enough if he were

---

[1] 218. 12–5, cf. 217. 18 f., though Sansalas owned a house, 219. 5.

[2] 217. 27: see p. 71 n. 2 above. There is no reason to believe that the martyr Nicetas (if he ever existed) was an optimate: see Delehaye, 282.

willing to eat *any* meat. When no persecution was on foot Christian and pagan seem to have lived on friendly terms within the one village; and in times of persecution, if we may generalize from the behaviour of Saba's fellow-villagers, regard for one's neighbour was stronger than differences of religion among the rank and file of the Visigoths. The brotherly and sisterly intimacy of the Christians in Gothia is reflected in the diminutive names by which they addressed one another. As a German scholar has put it, the names of practically all the martyrs, in so far as they are Germanic, are 'Kurznamen, Kosenamen, Beinamen, oder Spitznamen'. But no 'Kosenamen' are applied to chiefs like Atharid or Winguric or even the Christian Arimerius (p. 159 below), who is known from a somewhat later period.[1] The simplicity of these lowly Christians and their earnest truthfulness are reflected in the one document that they have left us, the *Passion*.[2] It is not the work of a barbarian but of a Roman living in very close contact with the barbarians; and although it was scarcely written by the priest Sansalas himself, it may well be based on information supplied by him, for he had friends in the Roman Empire, had fled there when the persecution was at its height, and may well have returned there after Saba's death to await the end of the storm.[3] The vividness and innocence of the *Passion* reveal a community in which fanaticism was confined to the powerful, and humanity to the humble. Delehaye has justly described it as one of the pearls of ancient hagiography.

[1] Loewe, in the second of the articles cited on p. 69 n. 2 above, at 432 f.
[2] Whether the *Passion* is a reply to Basil, *Ep.* clv seems to me very doubtful: *contra*, J. Mansion, 'Les origines du Christianisme chez les Gots', *Analecta Bollandiana*, xxxiii (1914), 5–30, at 12.
[3] 218. 24, cf. Delehaye, 291.

77

CHAPTER FOUR

THE DATE OF THE CONVERSION

WHEN the Visigoths crossed the Danube in 376 and entered the Roman provinces, were they Christian or pagan? Were the two armies which clashed at Adrianople on 9 August 378 composed substantially of Christians, or were the victors still pagan? When Ulfila died in 381-3, had he succeeded in converting his fellow-countrymen to Christianity?

They had moved into Transdanubian Dacia when Aurelian withdrew the legions and the administrative personnel in the seventies of the third century (pp. 3 ff. above); but they did not thereby move into a Christian environment. No evidence has yet been identified to show that Christianity had gained a foothold in Dacia by the year 270;[1] and though it would be rash to deny that there were *any* Christians among the native population or among the soldiers, officials, and traders who came into the country, yet the bulk of the Romano-Dacian people was only converted to Christianity after the official Roman withdrawal.

Archaeology has revealed a number of Christian objects which date from the fourth century. They consist for the most part of terracotta lamps and funerary monuments. There was also found at Potaissa

---

[1] C. Daicoviciu, 'Există Monumente Creștine în Dacia Traiană din sec. ii–iii?', *Anuarul Institutului de Studii Classice*, ii (1934–5), 192–209, discusses with illustrations the alleged archaeological evidence; more briefly idem, 'Au sujet des monuments chrétiens de la Dacie Trajane', *Mélanges J. Marouzeau* (Paris, 1948), 119–24. The literary evidence is discussed by D. M. Pippidi, 'Intorno alle Fonti Letterarie del Cristianesimo Daco-Romano', *Revue historique du sud-est européen*, xx (1943), 166–81.

an interesting onyx intaglio inscribed with the word
IXΘYΣ and depicting the Good Shepherd carrying a
lamb, a tree with a dove seated upon it, and Jonah
falling from his ship into the sea in which a whale is
swimming.[1] Again, a bronze disc, which was found at
the village of Biertan in the county of Târnava Mare,
is perforated so as to form the words 'ego Zenovius
votum posui' and was discovered along with a bronze
plaque forming the Christian monogram *XP*.[2] Now, it is
noteworthy that these and the other Christian finds have
all been discovered in what had formerly been Roman
settlements—at Ampelum, Napoca, Apulum, and so
on[3]—and that no such objects have come from Wallachia, Moldavia, or Bessarabia or from the land between
the Danube and the Tisza which the Romans had not
occupied. They have been found only in what had once
been Romanized country. It is true that the objects in
question are few, but in view of the fact that they have

[1] D. Mitrea, 'O Gemă Creştină din Turda', *Revista Istorică Română*, xvi
(1946), 51–62.
[2] *CIL* iii. 1617, with K. Horedt, 'Eine lateinische Inschrift des 4.
Jahrhunderts aus Siebenbürgen', *Anuarul* (as above), iv (1941), 10–17;
I. Barnea, 'Contribuţii la Studiul Creştinismului in Dacia', *Revista
Istorică Română*, xiii (1942–3), 31–42, at 32 ff.; A. Alföldi, 'Eine lateinische
christliche Inschrift aus Siebenbürgen', *Archaeologiai Ertesitö*, Ser. iii,
vol. iii (1942), 255–8, though there is no need to suppose that this was an
article of plunder brought home from the Roman provinces, for this
supposition will not explain the peculiar distribution of the Christian
finds in Dacia.
[3] The pear-shaped Christian lamp found in or near Apulum is thought
by B. Mitrea, 'Une lampe chrétienne découverte en Transylvanie',
Dacia, ix–x (1941–4), 507–11, to date from the fourth century (though
the fifth is not impossible) and to have belonged to Romano-Dacians. If
it was in fact found in the Roman city it is not likely to have been
Visigothic, for there is neither evidence nor likelihood that the barbarians
occupied the Roman cities. For another lamp of similar date but without
Christian symbols, which is also thought to have been found at Apulum,
see K. Horedt, 'Funde der Völkerwanderungszeit aus Siebenbürgen',
Anuarul (as above), iv (1941), 163–79, at 165–7. Yet another Christian
lamp of the fourth century has been found at Mercheasa in the county
of Târnava Mare: ibid., 167.

all been discovered on Roman sites we are justified in assuming (at any rate until further evidence comes to hand) that these objects belonged not to Visigothic Christians but to Romano-Dacians who had been converted to the official Roman religion.[1] It is scarcely probable that they can all have belonged to the descendants of the Christian Roman prisoners who had been captured by the Goths in the great raids of the mid-third century, for otherwise the distribution of the finds would presumably have been different: the prisoners would not all have been put to work in the ruins of the old Roman cities. If it is true, then, that numbers of the Romano-Dacians were converted to Christianity early in the fourth century (for, as we have mentioned, there is no trace of Christianity in Dacia in the third century), can we specify the circumstances in which the conversion took place? The fifth-century ecclesiastical historians Socrates and Sozomen date the conversion of the Visigoths to the seventies of the fourth century, but they contradict both themselves and all other authorities by also dating the conversion to approximately 332. In that year the armies of Constantine the Great inflicted a heavy defeat on the Visigoths north of the Danube (p. 12 above), and 'they [i.e. the Visigoths] dismayed by the unexpectedness of the defeat believed then for the first time in the Christian religion, by which Constantine, too, was saved.'[2] What is the explanation of this double conversion of the Visigoths in the works of the two historians? Since we know that a substantial number of the Romano-Dacians were converted early in the fourth century—

---

[1] C. Daicoviciu, *La Transylvanie dans l'antiquité* (Bucharest, 1945), 223.

[2] Socrates, i. 18. 4; cf. Sozomen, ii. 6. 1. If this were true, it would certainly have been mentioned by Eusebius, *Vita Const.* iv. 5.

for otherwise the archaeological evidence is scarcely intelligible—may it not have been the case that Constantine's victory, in some way which cannot now be defined, resulted in a number of the Romano-Dacians going over to Christianity? Be that as it may, we may safely conclude that the environment which the Visigoths entered in the third century was not a Christian one but that to some extent it became Christian during the fourth century.

The Visigoths themselves, however, had been exposed to some Christian influence ever since the time of their great raids into the Roman provinces in the middle of the third century before they finally entered Dacia. They had then brought back with them numbers of prisoners from Asia Minor, particularly from Phrygia, Galatia, and Cappadocia.[1] They had brought their prisoners to southern Russia, for at the time of the raids they had not occupied Dacia; but presumably they transferred them, or some of them, to their new land. Now, these captive men and women were Christian in at least some cases—indeed, there was a number of clergy among them—and their descendants had remained Christians; and these prisoners converted some of their captors.[2] Their number was no doubt increased by prisoners taken in later raids on the Balkan provinces. Ulfila himself was descended on one side of his family from Cappadocian prisoners who had been carried off from their village of Sadagolthina near Parnassus; and Ulfila's successor as bishop of the Goths, a certain Selenas, was the son of a Gothic father and a Phrygian mother, and his name is thought to be

---

[1] Philostorgius, ii. 5 (p. 17. 5, ed. Bidez); Syncellus, p. 716, ed. Bonn; cf. Zosimus, i. 28. 1.
[2] Philostorgius, loc. cit.; Sozomen, ii. 6. 2.

81

Phrygian.[1] There were other Christian influences besides that of the prisoners and the Romano-Dacians. A number of missionaries are known to have gone into Gothia from the Roman provinces. A certain Eutyches, who can scarcely have lived much later than the early years of Constantius II, was a Cappadocian Catholic; and it was he, according to Basil of Caesarea, who sowed the seeds of Catholicism among the Visigoths.[2] Moreover, it would seem that Latin- as well as Greek-speaking missionaries had been working in Gothia before the days of Ulfila.[3] Finally, the aged schismatic, Audius of Mesopotamia, when exiled by Constantius II to the province of Scythia Minor (the Dobrogea), crossed the frontier, went into the interior of Gothia, made 'many' converts there among the Visigoths, and founded monasteries and convents.[4] He appointed

---

[1] Philostorgius, p. 17. 17; Socrates, v. 23. 8; cf. Sozomen, vii. 17. 12. On Selenas's name see R. Loewe, 'Der gotische Kalender', *ZfdA*, lix (1922), 245–90, at 277.

[2] Basil, *Ep.* 164, where τῇ ὑπομνήσει τῶν παλαιῶν is the only indication of Eutyches' date. See Scott, op. cit. (on p. xiv n. 1 above), 29 f.; M. H. Jellinek, *Geschichte der gotischen Sprache* (Berlin and Leipzig, 1926), 8.

[3] W. Schultze, *Kleine Schriften* (Göttingen, 1934), 513; Jellinek, op. cit., 188 ff., and 'Zur christlichen Terminologie im Gothischen', *Beiträge*, xlvii (1923), 434–47. Nothing can be deduced about early Visigothic Christianity from Tertullian, *adv. Iud.* vii: see Pippidi, art. cit. Athanasius, *Or. de Incarn. Verbi*, li, writing between 319 and 321, lists the Goths among those barbarians who had been reached by the Gospel. But that is not to say that they were then predominantly Christian, and moreover the Goths to whom he refers may be the Ostrogoths of the Crimea. Also, it is not at all certain that the Theophilus who was present at the Council of Nicaea was a Visigoth rather than an Ostrogoth. The *Vita* of Nicetas has little historical value so far as the Visigoths are concerned: see Delehaye, 285 f., where the reason for the author's false association of Ulfila with Theophilus is accounted for. See p. 164 below. On the other hand, Philostorgius, ii. 5, describes Ulfila as the first bishop of the Visigoths (though admittedly it is possible that he may mean the first Arian bishop).

[4] Epiphanius, *Panar. Haeres.* lxx (iii. 233, 247, ed. Holl); cf. Jerome, *Chron.* s.a. 341 (i. 453). L. Iselin, 'Audios und die Audianer', *Jahrbücher für protestantische Theologie*, xvi (1890), 298–305, disproves the suggestion

several bishops in Gothia, but we do not know that they were Goths. An unfortunate lacuna in the text of Epiphanius has robbed us of one or more of their names, and the only Audian bishop whose name has survived is Silvanus, who is not likely to have been a Visigoth.[1] At any rate, our authority distinctly implies that some of the Visigoths themselves entered the Audian monasteries and that the monasteries were not recruited exclusively from the descendants of the Roman prisoners.[2] These are the first monks of whom we happen to hear in Gothia; but there may well have been Catholic monasteries as early as those of Audius, for 'Harpyla a monk' figures in the list of those martyred in 372, and Harpyla was certainly a Visigoth, as his name shows.[3]

But in spite of all this Christian endeavour and in spite of the successes of Audius and others, the fact remains that *c.* 370 the Visigothic Christians were few and far between. Our most valuable authority on the subject is the *Passion of St. Saba*, which makes it clear that Saba and his fellow-believers formed nothing like a majority of the tribesmen during the Visigothic persecutions of the Christians in their midst in 369–72. Saba, we are told, lived 'in the midst of a crooked and perverted generation'.[4] When the members of his

once put forward tentatively by A. Harnack, *Theologische Literaturzeitung,* xi (1886), 77, that Audius was a Goth and bore a Gothic name.
[1] Epiphanius, loc. cit., 247 f. On the other hand, the Silvanus who was one of the signatories of the Burgundian *Liber Constitutionum* is believed to have borne a Germanic name by R. Kögel, 'Die Stellung des burgundischen innerhalb der germanischen Sprachen', *ZfdA,* xxxvii (1893), 223–31, at 229, who says that *silva* = Gothic *silba* = OHG *selbo.* But we need hardly discuss this suggestion.
[2] Epiphanius, loc. cit., 247. 29 f.
[3] Delehaye, 279. For an Ostrogothic monastery in the Eastern Empire in 404 see John Chrysostom, *Ep.* xiv.
[4] *Passion,* 216. 30.

village wished to tell the persecutors that there were no Christians in their village, Saba refused to allow them to do so; and the villagers swore therefore that there was but one, Saba himself, among them. In fact, there were others besides Saba;[1] but could the villagers possibly have sworn thus if a majority or even a considerable minority had been Christian? In the third wave of the persecution Saba and the priest Sansalas appear to have been the only persons who were molested in their village, and there is no reason for thinking that they were singled out from an extensive group of Christians for special treatment by the authorities. At the same time, when Sansalas had left his village and had fled to the Roman Empire for safety, Saba had no companion with whom to celebrate Easter and was, therefore, obliged to travel to the priest Guththica in a neighbouring village for company.[2] Other Christian documents tell a similar tale. When the persecutors burned a church over the heads of a Christian congregation in 370 a number of persons perished. But the names of 22 of them have survived, and the great majority of these names are thought not to be Gothic at all: some are Roman, some are believed to be Phrygian, Cappadocian, and Syrian.[3] If these 22

[1] Ibid., 218. 10, cf. 217. 30, 218. 9.

[2] Ibid., 218. 16 ff. The ἄλλοις πλείοσι of 218. 35 are not necessarily Christians. Incidentally, the existence of this name Guththica seems to have been overlooked by the commentators on the inscription conveniently printed by O. Fiebiger, *Inschriftensammlung zur Geschichte der Ostgermanen*, Zweite Folge, Akad. der Wissenschaften in Wien: phil.-hist. Klasse, Denkschriften Bd. 72, Abh. 2 (Vienna, 1944), 19 f., (no. 20), where we hear of a German named Herminarius who was *praepositus gentilium* at Inak in southern Syria in 208 with a son named Γούθθα. The name of our presbyter suggests that it is unnecessary to take the son's name to be non-Germanic or a stone-mason's error for *Guda* or *Gudda*.

[3] L. Schmidt, *Geschichte der deutschen Stämme: die Ostgermanen* (Munich, 1934), 235; H. Giesecke, *Die Ostgermanen und der Arianismus* (Leipzig and Berlin, 1939), 67. For the names see esp. H. Achelis, 'Der älteste deutsche

persons were typical of the Christians who could be found in Gothia in 370, then only a minority of those Christians were Visigoths. The people who bore non-Gothic names were presumably Roman prisoners or their descendants or an occasional Dacian, for there is neither evidence nor likelihood that any Visigoth living in Gothia at this date would have borne a non-Gothic name (though this is not so of East Germans who had migrated into the Roman provinces). Finally, as late as the joint reign of Valentinian II and Theodosius (383–92) a Visigothic Christian named Wella was stoned to death for his religion in spite of the fact that he was a companion of the Christian queen Gaatha (p. 159 below). Even at that date the victory of Christianity was incomplete, and the pagans could still organize a violent outburst against it.[1] It is true that these documents portray a time of persecution when many Christians fled into the Roman Empire.[2] But few will object that the isolation of Saba, Sansalas, and Guththica pictured in the *Passion* means no more than that, when the persecution was at its height, only a few Christians remained behind in Gothia and that in more peaceful times these Christians would not have been so exceedingly isolated. There is no possibility, so far as I

Kalender', *Zeitschrift für die neutestamentliche Wissenschaft*, i (1900), 308–35, at 323, where there is a complete list of the MS. variants; and note Constans, ibid., 318. Sansalas also has an Asian name: Loewe, art. cit., 277 f., and 'Gotische Namen in hagiographischen Texten', *Beiträge*, xlvii (1923), 407–33, at 432. On the other hand, Saba is said to have been Γότθος τῷ γένει, and so also in the title of the *Passion*. The name *Saba* has usually been considered to be Germanic since K. Müllenhoff, *ZfdA*, vi (1848), 459, cf. xviii (1875), 255, and e.g. E. Förstemann, *Altdeutsches Namenbuch*, i² (Bonn, 1900), 1285 f., though this is not accepted by K. Helm, *Altgermanische Religionsgeschichte* (Heidelberg, 1937), ii. i. 72 n. 1, who admits, however, that he was Gothic by descent. Note that the East Saxon king Saberct was sometimes called Saba: Bede, *HE* ii. 5.

[1] Delehaye, 279.
[2] *Passion*, 218. 24; Orosius, vii. 32. 9; Jerome, *Chron.* s.a. 371.

can see, of proving that more than a tiny percentage of Visigoths fled to the Imperial provinces in 369–72; and when this handful was gone Saba and a few friends were left almost alone. On this supposition, and only on this, it may be suggested, is it possible to make sense of the conditions depicted in the various Visigothic *Passions*. The conversion of the great bulk of the Visigoths must therefore be dated to the time when they were no longer settled in Gothia: they were not yet a Christian people in the years before the devastating attack of the Huns was launched upon them in 376.[1]

A number of authors, who lived in the fifth and sixth centuries, date the conversion to the year 376 itself. Orosius says that at some date earlier than the battle of Adrianople in 378 the Goths (for no apparent reason) humbly sent to Valens asking him to supply them with 'bishops' from whom they could learn the rule of the Christian faith. Valens, being an accursed Arian, sent them Arian teachers, and hence the Goths became and remained Arians. It was accordingly a just judgement of God that they should have burned Valens alive at Adrianople, for it is because of him that they themselves are destined to burn for their heresy in the world that is to come.[2] Orosius does not give an exact date for the Goths' request for these bishops; but perhaps he intends us to understand that the request was made about the year 376. Certainly that was how Jordanes understood the tale (which he repeats with embellishments), for he dates the request to the time when the Visigoths were about to be attacked by the Huns, that is, to the year

---

[1] For positive evidence of Visigothic paganism before 376 Pippidi, art. cit., 176–81, is inclined to refer to Macarius of Magnesia, *Apocrit.* iv. 13 (in C. Blondel, *Macarii Magnetis quae supersunt* (Paris, 1876), 179), but the reference there is to the nomadic peoples of the steppe region.

[2] Orosius, vii. 33. 19.

376; and Valens sent the teachers after the barbarians had crossed the river Danube in the same year.[1] The story is a naive attempt to account for the Arianism of the Visigoths: but has it any foundation in fact?

Among the Greek writers a different account is found. Socrates and Sozomen give a more elaborate explanation of the Visigoths' Arianism than that which had satisfied Orosius and was later to satisfy Jordanes. According to Socrates, a civil war had broken out among the Visigoths before the persecution of the Christians in 369–72, Athanaric leading one faction and Fritigern the other. Fritigern appealed to the Romans for help, and it was with the aid of Roman armed force that his party was able to win the war against Athanaric. As a mark of gratitude to Valens, therefore, Fritigern and his followers adopted that Emperor's faith. Socrates dated this story to a time before 369, but he was at once criticized by Sozomen for doing so; and the reason for Sozomen's criticism is not difficult to divine. If the civil war and Athanaric's defeat had taken place in or before 369, how had it come about that Athanaric and not Fritigern was the Visigothic leader at the beginning of the campaign against the Huns in 376? Accordingly, Sozomen transfers the whole story of the alleged civil war and the resultant conversion to the time when the Visigoths had crossed the Danube and were now inside the Empire, that is, to late in the year 376, the year which appears to have been favoured by the Latin writers. Unhappily, he then found himself in a difficulty no less perplexing than that which had tripped up Socrates; for the form in which he tells the story made it necessary for him to transfer Athanaric's persecution from 369–72 to the same date, 376, which

[1] Jordanes, *Get.* xxv. 131 f.

is impossible.[1] The fact is that it is difficult to find a precise date for an event which never took place.

The whole story of the alleged civil war and the appeal to Valens for Christian teachers should be dismissed as a fabrication designed to account for the Arianism of the Visigoths. In the first place, there is no evidence for the civil war outside the pages of Socrates and Sozomen, whose accounts are self-contradictory and whose works are insecure authorities for events which took place outside the northern frontier of the Empire.[2] Secondly, the silence of the fourth-century authors and especially of Ammianus Marcellinus is decisive. Ammianus gives as the reason for Valens' attack on the Visigoths in 367 the fact that the Emperor learned from the reports of his frontier commanders that the Visigoths were conspiring together and making preparations to invade the frontier districts of Thrace (p. 17 above).[3] Now, the war would have been a signal success for the Romans if it had left the Visigoths, so far from federating their tribes, actually engaged in a bitter civil war. But Ammianus gives no hint that this was the case. If we are to believe Socrates and Sozomen we must be prepared to convict Ammianus of having given a grossly inadequate account of the results of the Romano-Gothic war of 367-9 and indeed of having missed altogether the significance of the struggle. But before we can bring such an accusation against an historian of Ammianus' calibre we shall require some better authority than that of Socrates and Sozomen. Thirdly,

[1] Socrates, iv. 33; Sozomen, vi. 37. 6 ff.; cf. John of Antioch, frag. 184. 2. The evidence of Theodoret and Isidore of Seville need not be discussed.

[2] J. Mansion, 'Les origines du Christianisme chez les Gots', *Analecta Bollandiana*, xxxiii (1914), 5-30, at 24.

[3] Amm. Marc., xxvi. 6. 11. Unfortunately, Lippold, P.-W. ix. A1. 519 f., does not discuss this point.

the two ecclesiastical writers ask us to believe that Athanaric was the military leader of the Visigoths in 367–9, that he was shortly afterwards replaced by Fritigern as a result of the civil war, that he reappeared as leader against the Huns in 376, and that he was again replaced by Fritigern in the autumn of that year. But this argues an instability and fickleness in Visigothic society which we cannot lightly assume in any of the primitive Germanic peoples.

The reason why the legend of the civil war and the appeal to Valens came into existence in the first place is not difficult to explain. In 376 Athanaric was indeed replaced by Fritigern, though not because of a civil war: hence the alleged conflict inside Visigothic society in which Fritigern was said to have fought and defeated Athanaric.[1] Again, the Visigoths were in fact converted to Arianism at approximately this time: hence the association of the conversion with Valens, who was an ardent Arian. The whole story was designed to explain the fact that the Visigoths were converted not to Catholicism but to Arianism.

Finally, the evidence given by St. Ambrose is irreconcilable with the story told by Socrates and Sozomen and also with that of Orosius. Indeed, it is hardly credible that if there had been a dramatic conversion in 376 Ambrose would have given no indication of it in the passages where he refers to the religion of the Visigoths. When he refers incidentally to the matter in 378 he implies that the barbarians were pagan.[2] A few years later, in 381, he is quite explicit: the Visigoths are still a pagan people and it is

[1] For the circumstances in which the Visigoths actually abandoned Athanaric see Amm. Marc. xxxi. 3. 8.

[2] Ambrose, de Fide, ii. 16. 140 sacrilegis vocibus. On the date see F. Homes Dudden, The Life and Times of St. Ambrose (Oxford, 1935), ii. 698.

sacrilege for a Christian priest to wear a necklace and armbands like those of the idolatrous Gothic priests.[1] It is not until we come to the *Expositio Evangelii sec. Lucam*[2] that we find that Ambrose regards the Visigoths as a Christian people. Unfortunately, the date of the relevant parts of that work is obscure, and we can say no more than that the words in question may have been written as late as *c.* 390.[3] In short, not one of our fourth-century authorities, Ammianus, Themistius, Ambrose, or Auxentius (for whom see below) knows anything of a spectacular conversion either in 376 or at any other time: and they supply us with no evidence to suggest that the bulk of the Visigoths were converted before the treaty of 3 October 382, by the terms of which the Roman authorities settled them as Federates in Moesia. But, as Ambrose shows, it was possible to refer to them as a Christian people within a decade of the settlement in Moesia.

After the Visigoths left Moesia in 395 Roman writers always speak of them as Christian. The first to do so appears to be St. Jerome who in a letter in 403 states

---

[1] *Ep.* x. 9, of which the best text will be found in R. Egger, 'Die Zerstörung Pettaus durch die Goten', *Jahreshefte d. österreichischen Instituts in Wien*, xviii (1915), Beiblatt 253–66. On the date see Dudden, op. cit., i. 201, n. 2. We are not concerned, of course, with those Goths who deserted the bulk of their countrymen and took service with the Romans: see e.g. Ambrose, *Ep.* xx. 12; Zosimus, iv. 25. 2 f.; Gregory of Nazianzus, *Ep.* cxxxvi f. (Migne, *PG* xxxvii. 322); and Gainas.

[2] ii. 37, x. 14.

[3] The arguments of J. Palanque, *St. Ambroise et l'empire romain* (Paris, 1933), 529 ff., and of Dudden, op. cit., ii. 692 ff., are wholly inconclusive in so far as Books ii and x of this work are concerned: they both assume that the Visigoths were Christian in 377. No evidence for Visigothic Arianism can be found in Gregory of Nazianzus, *Or.* xxxiii. 2 (Migne, *PG* xxxvi. 216) of A.D. 380, on which see F. Jostes, 'Das Todesjahr des Ulfilas und der Übertritt der Goten zum Arianismus', *Beiträge*, xxii (1897), 158–87, at 177 f. I confess that I do not know what to make of Eunapius, frag. 55, but I take it that no one would claim on the strength of that passage that Eunapius believed the Visigoths to have been Christian in 376.

that the Goths can fight on equal terms with the Romans and suggests that this may be so because they subscribe to a similar religion.[1] His statement is supported by an anonymous preacher who delivered a sermon in Edessa at about the same time as Jerome's letter was written. This preacher apparently believed that the majority of the Visigoths had been converted to Arianism by the opening years of the fifth century; and it is interesting that the news of the conversion was familiar in so distant a part of the Eastern provinces in the reign of the Emperor Arcadius.[2] And Orosius and others are very emphatic in asserting that it was a Christian army which captured Rome in 410. Indeed, Augustine says that the Visigoths were the enemies of idols and fought far more bitterly against the pagan gods and unhallowed sacrifices than they did against men.[3] It would therefore be consistent with the evidence to suppose that the conversion must be dated to the period of the settlement in Moesia, that is, to the years 382–95. The questions why they should have altered their religious beliefs precisely then rather than sooner or later, and why they should have begun to subscribe to Arianism rather than to Catholicism, are problems which we shall try to tackle in the next chapter.

It must not be thought, of course, that every vestige of pagan belief and practice disappeared overnight from among the Visigoths. We shall see (p. 159 below) that the pagans were capable of organizing a violent

---

[1] *Ep.* cvii. 2. It is true that the passage is somewhat tendentious, but Jerome would not have used the words 'quia pari religione confidunt' of a pagan people.

[2] *Sermo in S. Thomam*, etc. (Migne, *PG* lix. 500).

[3] Orosius, vii. 37. 2, cf. 39. 1; Augustine, *De Civ. Dei*, v. 23, *Sermo* cv. 10. 13 (Migne, *PL* xxxviii. 625). For a Visigothic optimate who was a Christian in 410 see Orosius, vii. 39. 3, and for an Arian see Sozomen, ix. 10. 1.

attack on a Christian in the period 383–92, the very period to which we have assigned the conversion in general. And the manner of Alaric's burial was by no means typically Christian: his followers buried him in the river Basentus in southern Italy, diverted its waters into another channel, and massacred the men who had carried out the work.[1] Indeed, for many generations, even for centuries, after the official conversion pagan survivals could be found among them; but there is little detailed information. It would be interesting to know more about those songs which the Visigothic warriors sang over the body of King Theodoric I when they found it on the Catalaunian Plains on the morrow of the victory over Attila in 451.[2] They were songs in praise of the dead warrior and were accompanied in the funeral procession by the clashing of weapons. They may or may not have had a distinctively pagan character. But the bishops assembled at the Third Council of Toledo in 589 found it necessary to declare that psalms alone should be sung at the funerals of Christian priests and not the baneful song which is commonly sung by the people over the dead; nor should men slash their own breasts or those of their kinsmen or of their family.[3] At the Council of Narbonne held in that same year the bishops were aghast to learn that many Catholics considered Thursday to be Jupiter's day and would do no work upon it. They enacted that free persons who refused to work on a Thursday in future should be excluded from the Church and should spend a year in

[1] Jordanes, *Get.* xxx. 158. The truth of his story is unnecessarily contested by e.g. S. Reinach, *Cultes, Mythes, et Religions* (Paris, 1923), v. 286–92: see A. van Gennep, 'La tombe d'Alaric', *Revue archéologique*, Ser. v, vol. xix (1924), 195–207. The killing of the prisoners may have been a sacrifice to the dead: Helm, op. cit., 16 f.
[2] Jordanes, *Get.* xli. 214.
[3] J. Mansi, *Conc. Coll.* ix. 998 f., canon 22.

penance, while slaves who did so should be beaten.[1] Even in the seventh century the bishops of the Visigothic kingdom in Spain were still worried by paganism.[2] Unfortunately, we do not know to what extent the various pagan practices to which our sources refer were traditional among the Visigoths or had been altered or had even been acquired as a result of the Visigoths' entering the Roman Empire; nor do we know whether or to what extent the magic of the Visigoths differed from that of the Roman populations by which they were surrounded.

If we date the conversion of the Visigoths to the years 382–95 we can see why it is that Auxentius in his famous account of Ulfila's career never claims that the great man had converted his fellow-countrymen to Christianity. Auxentius could not have made such a claim, for in fact the Visigoths were still substantially pagan when Ulfila died in 381–3. The Apostle of the Goths did not convert the Goths to Christianity.

[1] Ibid., 1,018, canon 15.
[2] See S. McKenna, *Paganism and Pagan Survivals in Spain up to the Fall of the Visigothic Kingdom* (Washington, 1938).

CHAPTER FIVE

EARLY VISIGOTHIC CHRISTIANITY

IF we agree, then, that the general conversion of the Visigoths was brought about while they were settled in Moesia in the years 382–95, we may turn to somewhat wider questions. In the following pages I propose to discuss (i) the fourth-century persecutions; (ii) the circumstances of the conversion; (iii) Visigothic ecclesiastical organization; (iv) Ulfila's achievement; (v) the works of the Arian bishop Maximinus, practically the only books which enable us to gain some insight into the character of Visigothic Christianity; and (vi) the general question of the conversion of the barbarians to Christianity.

1. The Fourth-Century Persecutions

Here is a summary of what is known of Visigothic Christianity as it was in the year 369 on the eve of the second persecution. The Christians at that date were divided into at least three sects. First, there was a number of followers of the schismatic, if not heretical, Audius; and the piety, austerity, and virtue of the Audians reached such heights as to win praise even from a Catholic writer. Audius founded monasteries and convents in Gothia, and these were not recruited solely from Roman prisoners: some Visigoths entered them, too.[1] It is unlikely that the sect survived for long in Gothia after the persecution of 369–72. The majority of its adherents fled to the eastern provinces of the

---

[1] Epiphanius, *Panar, Haeres.* 247 (pp. 29 ff., ed. Holl).

Eastern Roman Empire, and the sparse remnants were probably absorbed into Catholicism rather than into Arianism, for they were far closer in doctrine to the Catholics than to the Arians, as our authority repeatedly emphasizes.[1] Secondly, there were the Arians, a number of whom, though not all, fled into the Roman provinces with Ulfila in 347–8. Only one of them apart from Ulfila is known by name—the martyr Frederic who is mentioned in the Gothic Calendar (p. 157 below)—but even an orthodox writer concedes that Arians, too, were among the martyrs of 369–72.[2] Finally, there were the Catholics, of whom St. Saba was the most eminent, though it would seem that in the middle of the fourth century they had also a bishop named Godda (pp. 161 ff. below). It is commonly believed that the twenty-six persons who were burned in a church during the persecution were Catholics; and Nicetas was a Catholic, of whom we otherwise know little.[3] Monasticism had won a footing among the Catholics as well as among the Audians.[4]

Unfortunately, there is no means of knowing which of these sects had won the greatest number of adherents before 376; but what seems to be certain is that in that year there were not many Christians of any description in Gothia. Such Christians as existed there were

[1] Ibid., 248. 18, 25 f., cf. J. Mansion, 'Les origines du Christianisme chez les Gots', *Analecta Bollandiana*, xxxiii (1914), 5–30, at 7. Closer to Catholicism: Epiphanius, 230. 2 f., 233. 21 f., 26, 29, who, perhaps generously, regards them as schismatics rather than heretics, 230. 4.

[2] Socrates, iv. 33. 7.

[3] On the sect of the 26 martyrs see Mansion, art. cit. 24–30, followed by J. Zeiller, *Les origines chrétiennes dans les provinces danubiennes*, (Paris, 1918), 434–6; Assunta Nagl, P.-W. Vll A, 2119. That they were Arians is argued by R. Loewe, 'Der gotische Kalender', *ZfdA*, lix (1922), 245–90, at 265–7. Inna, Rema, and Pinna seem to have been Catholic: pp. 161 ff. below.

[4] Harpyla was a Visigoth, as his name shows: Delehaye, 279.

scattered up and down the country, a handful in this village and a handful in that; and they appear to have belonged to the poorest strata of Visigothic society. There is no reason to suppose that any of the optimates had as yet been touched by the new religion, and in 369 it was 'the megistanes throughout Gothia' who ordered the Christians in the country to be persecuted. Before 376 Christianity in Gothia was essentially an affair of the poor. Yet in spite of their dangers and difficulties the Gothic Christians tried to convert their fellow-Goths,[1] and they even sent out missionaries to their kinsmen, the Ostrogoths in the Ukraine and the Gepids in the mountains north of Transylvania, preaching the Gospel and trying to win them to the faith.[2] But both at home and abroad their efforts met with little success, and the barbarians of south-eastern Europe were still overwhelmingly pagan when the Huns arrived there and the Visigoths crossed the Danube in 376.

The followers of Ulfila and Saba paid a heavy price for worshipping the foreign God in the tents which served them as churches.[3] Their numbers doubtless grew in the seven years following 341, when Ulfila returned to Gothia after being consecrated bishop by Eusebius of Nicomedia. But in 347–8 came the first persecution in Gothia, and 'many' men and women were martyred.[4] Ulfila at the head of an 'immense people' fled from Gothia,[5] was welcomed into the Roman Empire by Constantius II, and was provided with land around the Moesian city of Nicopolis; and

---

[1] *Passio SS. Innae*, etc.: Delehaye, 216. 1.

[2] Jordanes, *Get.* xxv. 133.

[3] Sozomen, vi. 37. 13 f.; Jerome. *Ep.* cvii. 2.

[4] Auxentius, 75. 27: 'ubi et post multorum servorum et ancillarum Cristi gloriosum martyrium'.

[5] Ibid., 29 'cum grandi populo confessorum'; Philostorgius, ii. 5 πολὺν λαόν; Jordanes, *Get.* li. 267 *populus inmensus*; cf. Zeiller, op. cit. 420, n. 3.

there is no evidence that he ever returned to Gothia. Now, the number of those who crossed the Danube with him was undoubtedly small, and phrases about the 'immense people' who accompanied him into exile are devout and patriotic exaggerations. The persecution apparently affected Catholics as well as Arians, but it made little impression on contemporary Romans. Although Constantius used to call Ulfila 'the Moses of our time', only one contemporary Roman writer makes an incidental reference to the persecution, and none at all speaks of the exodus from Gothia.[1]

There is no reason to believe that every Christian in Gothia fled with Ulfila in 347–8, and the number of those who remained behind may well have increased by the time of the Emperor Valens' campaigns in Gothia in 367–9. The second persecution was ordered by the megistanes on the morrow of the defeat by Valens in 369, and was enforced by the confederate chief Athanaric[2] and by the tribal chieftains. It was carried out in three waves, and Saba was martyred on 12 April 372 after he had survived the two earlier outbreaks.[3] In the intervals between the three outbursts there was comparative peace, and Christians who had

---

[1] Cyril of Jerusalem, *Catech.* x. 19 (Migne, *PG* xxxiii. 687), who presumably has Catholic martyrs in mind. Philostorgius, ii. 6 ὁ ἐφ' ἡμῶν Μωσῆς, cf. Auxentius, 75. 31. Ulfila's hardships are referred to in Sozomen, vi. 37. 11.

[2] Jerome, *Chron.* s.a. 371 'de propriis sedibus in Romanum solum expellit' (sc. Haitanaricus); Orosius, vii. 32. 9.

[3] *Passion of St. Saba*, 217. 26, 218. 2 f., 16. In the second of these passages persecution is regarded as 'customary'. The 26 martyrs, for whom see also Sozomen, vi. 37. 14, died either on 26 March (so the Synaxaries) or on 29 October (so the Gothic Calendar) in the year 370. Loewe, loc. cit., discusses the chronology but would seem to press the evidence too far. I follow the customary usage in referring to the '26 martyrs'; but 27 are known, for we must not forget Constans (p. 84 n. 3 above). In fact, however, there were more even than 27, for the list of names is said explicitly to be a selection.

gone into hiding or had taken refuge in the Roman provinces were able to return unmolested to their homes if they so wished.[1] The fate of those persecuted on this occasion created a deep impression on Roman Christians.[2] But many escaped into the Empire,[3] the Arians presumably joining Ulfila's settlement at Nicopolis, the Catholics founding a new community of their own somewhere south of the Danube (p. 103 below), and many of the Audians fleeing to distant Chalcis near Antioch and to places south of the Euphrates; while some Christians continued in their faith in Gothia itself even after the persecution, for by no means all the Christians in Gothia had revealed their Christianity to the persecutors.[4]

Why did the council of the megistanes order the persecution in the first place? Of the causes of the outbreak of 347–8 nothing whatever is known, but our authorities mention two motives in connexion with that of 369–72. According to the ecclesiastical historian Socrates, the persecution was enforced 'because the ancestral religion was being debased'. This reason, which the historian says motivated Athanaric, is plausible as far as it goes.[5] Athanaric appears to have been a staunch leader, 'the very type', it has been said, 'of stern, morose adherence to old Gothic ways'.[6] He

[1] *Passion*, 218. 2, 24 f.

[2] Basil, *Ep.* 155 *fin.*, 164 (where τὸ ξύλον, τὸ ὕδωρ refers to the fate of Saba); Epiphanius, loc. cit.; Ambrose, *Expos. Evang. sec. Lucam*, ii. 37; Jerome, loc. cit.; Prosper, *Chron.* 1140; Augustine, *Civ. Dei* xviii. 52 (who had spoken to survivors); Pseudo-Chrysostom, *Sermo* i (Migne, *PG* lii. 808), 'antea Gotthi patres occidebant; hodie sanguinem suum pro pia religione fundere non dubitant'.

[3] Orosius, vii. 32. 9; Isidore, *Hist. Goth.* 6 (ii, 269 f.); cf. Jerome, loc. cit.

[4] Epiphanius, 248. 22 ff.; *Passion*, cap. iii.

[5] Socrates, iv. 33. 7; cf. Sozomen. vi. 37. 12.

[6] T. Hodgkin, *Italy and Her Invaders*, I. i. 168. For something like a tribute to Athanaric see Themistius, *Or.* x. 134 C.

was willing to continue the struggle against the Huns in 376 when the bulk of his countrymen preferred to flee to the Romans for protection. He had sworn a tremendous oath never to set foot on the soil of the traditional foe, Rome. When he had forbidden the Romans to call him 'king' instead of 'Judge', his proper title, he had refused to allow even the suspicion to arise that he was aiming at a personal despotism over his people (p. 46 above). Such a man is unlikely to have welcomed the sight of some of his people abandoning the old tribal beliefs and attaching themselves to a new religion, and a Roman one at that. Athanaric, we may be sure, carried out the orders of the megistanes with gusto; and some of the Visigoths who were discovered to have embraced Christianity were put to death by the old ritual method of drowning. The four Christians known to have been drowned in the persecution of 369–72 are all thought to bear Gothic names—Saba, Inna, Rema, and Pinna.[1] They were not of Roman descent but were all born Visigoths; and their offence—the abandoning of the religion of their clans—was more heinous than the offence of those Roman prisoners who had been converted to Christianity.

Even Socrates, who wrote more than half a century after the persecution, connects the outbreak with the political events which preceded it, fictitious though his account of those events may be (p. 87 f. above); and the only contemporary authority to refer to the motives of the persecutors, Epiphanius, who wrote only four years after the persecution, says simply that 'in order to spite the Romans, because the Emperors of the Romans were Christians, he drove out the whole race of Chris-

---

[1] On them see Delehaye, 279, 287.

tians from those regions'.[1] The Visigothic Christians
associated with persons bearing such names as Constans,
Nicetas, Anna, Dulcilla, and so on.[2] They so venerated
a Roman Emperor, Constantius II, who had welcomed
Ulfila in the days of his trouble, as to allot him a day in
their Calendar of Church feasts (and they are the only
Christian community which is known to have honoured
Constantius thus).[3] They were in close relations with
the Roman provinces of Asia Minor. In a moment of
danger they would flee to the hated Romans as to
brothers, and Valens had good political reasons for
allowing them to remain in the provinces.[4] At least one
of them, Saba, was unwilling to take part in a sacred
and traditional clan feast when called upon to do so,
and he tried to induce others to refrain likewise. The
confederate council in 369, still smarting under the
defeat inflicted by Valens, must have wondered
whether tribal loyalties still meant anything to such
men and women as these. On the other hand, it must
not be supposed that every Christian in Gothia looked
upon the Romans with a kindly eye: we shall see that
when the Visigoths crossed into the Empire in 376 their
warriors included some Christians who by no means

[1] Epiphanius, 248. 20. The Visigoths' hostility to the Romans after the
war of 367–9 is mentioned by Themistius, *Or.* xi. 148 D (A.D. 373).

[2] H. Achelis, 'Der älteste deutsche Kalender', *Zeitschrift für die neu-
testamentliche Wissenschaft*, i (1900), 308–35, at 318; Delehaye, 279. On
Constans, whose name appears to be preserved in one text only, see
Achelis, art. cit.; R. Loewe, 'Gotische Namen in hagiographischen
Texten', *Beiträge*, xlvii (1923), 407–33, at 408 ff.

[3] It is universally agreed that in the Gothic Calendar (at 3 November)
Kustanteinus thiudanis is a slip and that Constantius is meant: Achelis, art.
cit. 332; Delehaye, 276 f.; cf. Auxentius, 75. 30 'athuc beate memorie
Constantio principe'.

[4] Orosius, vii. 32. 9; cf. *Passion*, 218. 24; Loewe, art. cit. (on p. 95 n. 3
above), 277 f. Their close ties with Asia Minor are by no means wholly
disproved by M. H. Jellinek, *Festschrift Fr. Kluge* (Tübingen, 1926), 61–5:
see J. Mansion, 'A propos des Chrétientés de Gotie', *Analecta Bollandiana*,
xlvi (1928), 365 f.

favoured the Romans (p. 103 f. below). Yet it cannot be doubted that a substantial number of the Christians regarded the Romans as 'brothers' and to that extent justified the fears of the optimates in 369.

The evidence of our two sources, then, at least provides us with the pretexts for the persecution. The megistanes ordered the persecution of the Christians both as an anti-Roman measure, to halt the spread of Roman influence in Gothia, and at the same time so as to check the decay of the old tribal religion. If we wish to go beyond our sources in this matter, there is a further point which we might consider. We mentioned earlier the fact that the Visigothic tribal system was itself in a state of decay at this date. The old egalitarianism had broken down, the rich man was seizing power, and the poor man was now a political cipher in Gothia. I would suggest as an hypothesis that the decay of the tribal religion and the spread of Roman influence were both alike merely symptoms of the collapse of tribalism. If tribal life had still been in a healthy condition, its religion would not have been disintegrating and spiritual influences from the Roman Empire would not have been making much headway in Gothia. Tribal religion was an integral part of the tribal system itself: neither could exist in its old form without the other. But now the accumulation of privately owned wealth and the concentration of political power into comparatively few hands were putting an end to the significance of the tribes and hence to the religion of the tribes. That, we may think, is why paganism declined and Christianity triumphed in the last quarter of the century rather than sooner or later. If this suggestion is correct, it follows that the megistanes, when they persecuted the Christians, were punishing others for bringing about a situation which they themselves had involuntarily created.

At all events, the persecution was planned and enforced by the megistanes, while the people as a whole resisted it, or did without enthusiasm what they were ordered to do, or even tried to shelter their members from its blasts. This suggests that the megistanes may have had another reason for ordering the persecution than those which are reported by our authorities. Since the Christians were drawn in the main from the humblest parts of Visigothic society, the persecution launched by the megistanes was in fact an attack directed at a weak, small, and to some extent an isolated section of the poorer folk of Gothia. It would seem that if Saba had owned some substantial property, the persecutor might have been less ruthless in his treatment of him. I would suggest that the immediate reason for the persecution was a political one. In 367–9 the Visigothic optimates had led the people to starvation and defeat in the war with Valens; and it is scarcely credible that their inadequacy or ill-fortune as leaders had failed to call forth criticism from those whom they had led to hunger and ruin. The persecution, we may believe, was their answer to the criticisms, for it can hardly be a coincidence that it was on the very morrow of their defeat that they began to burn and drown numbers of the poorer men and women of Gothia. They tried (on this hypothesis) to divert the hostility of the common warriors from themselves to the small and helpless community of Christians. Saba and his companions may have been used as a scapegoat for the defeat of 369.

2. The Circumstances of the Conversion

When the Visigoths entered the Roman Empire they soon encountered two groups of Christian Visigoths who had already settled in the provinces before 376. One of these groups consisted of the followers of Ulfila, who had been driven from Gothia in 347–8 and were now living near the city of Nicopolis. They evidently refused to join the main body of their compatriots, even though these had occupied the region around Nicopolis and Beroea soon after they had entered the Empire.[1] They did not move even when Nicopolis opened its gates to the invaders in the early years of Theodosius I,[2] and they were still leading their meagre, semi-pastoral life in that same neighbourhood two hundred years later, forgotten until Jordanes noticed them.[3] The second of these groups of Christians who were settled in the Empire is known only from a brief entry in a seventh-century chronicle. In 378, we are told, the 'Gothic Confessors', who seem to be the Christians in Fritigern's army, came upon the 'former Goths', who had been driven from their country some time before on account of their faith, for they were Catholics (and so cannot be identified with Ulfila's followers). The Gothic Confessors asked these Catholics to join them in collecting booty from the Romans: presumably the 'former Goths' would be familiar with the countryside and so would be able to help their starving countrymen to find food. But, like Ulfila's followers, they refused.

---

[1] Amm. Marc., xxxi. 11. 2.   [2] Eunapius, frag. 50.
[3] Jordanes, *Get.* li. 267. I do not believe that they are to be identified with those Goths whose remains have been found in the forts excavated near Sadowetz: G. Bersu, 'A Sixth-Century German Settlement of *Foederati*: Golemanovo Kale', *Antiquity*, xii (1938), 31–43; H. Vetters, *Dacia Ripensis* (Vienna, 1950), 25, 56 f.

Hence the Confessors killed some of them, and the rest fled to the neighbouring mountains and persisted in their Catholicism and *in their friendship with the Roman government*, which had given them hospitality when they had been expelled from their homeland in the days of persecution.[1] The italicized words should be noted. It was the first occasion on which Christianity appears openly as the pro-Roman force which Athanaric had feared it might one day become. But Christianity was divided against itself. It was a pro-Roman force only among those groups of Visigoths who had received land from the Imperial government. Those who had not yet received land were as hostile to the Romans as were their pagan countrymen with whom they had crossed the Danube. Whatever bonds may have tended to unite the Visigothic Christians, there were other forces which were yet stronger and which could bring them into bitter conflict with one another.

The subtle diplomacy of Theodosius I, which had so striking an effect on the political life of the Visigoths, did not leave their religious life unchanged. The Emperor induced several of their leaders besides the pro-Roman Fravitta to abandon Gothic society altogether and to live among the Romans; and a number of the chiefs who were won over by him began to subscribe—whether or not with sincerity—to the religious beliefs of the Romans at the same time as they put on the uniform of the Roman army. Thus, Modares was now converted to Catholicism, and as early as the first months of 382 he had become a correspondant of Gregory of Nazianzus: he had only recently deserted

[1] Isidore, *Hist. Goth.* 10 (ii, 271 f.); Zeiller, op. cit. 437; idem, *Miscellanea Isidoriana: Homenaje a S. Isidoro de Sevilla* (Rome, 1936), 289–92. Independent evidence for Christianity in Fritigern's army will be found in Amm. Marc., xxxi. 12. 8 f.

the Visigoths, and he showed such fervent loyalty to the Romans that, after he received a command in the Roman army, he proceeded to inflict a sharp defeat on a raiding-party of his fellow-Visigoths.[1] Gainas became an Arian, and there is little reason to doubt that he did so at about the same time as he sided with Theodosius. But to attach oneself to the religion of the Romans did not necessarily involve becoming a Christian: many Romans were still pagan. Hence, Fravitta himself together with some of his adherents subscribed outspokenly to a form of paganism which won the enthusiastic approval of the Neoplatonist philosopher Eunapius. It is unlikely that Eunapius would have penned his eulogy of Fravitta's paganism if that paganism had been simply the primitive tribal religion of Athanaric; and Eunapius' language seems to imply that Fravitta and others had begun to worship, however perfunctorily and with however little understanding, at the old altars of Hellas.[2] As a parallel to this conversion of a German to Eastern pagan beliefs we may refer to an Alamannic optimate named Mederic who lived in Gaul as a hostage in the mid-fourth century and had been initiated there into the mysteries of Serapis. On his return to his people beyond the Rhine he changed the name of his son Agenaric to Serapio, and he retained his Eastern religion (or his smattering of it) even when no longer living in the Empire.[3] Again, a German of unknown origin named Sigismund, who died at Rome apparently in the fifth

[1] Zosimus, iv. 25. 2 f.; Greg. Naz., Ep. 136, cf. 137 (Migne, PG xxxvii. 232 f.). See the article cited on p. 24 n. 2 above.
[2] Eunapius, frag. 60 (252. 22 ff., 253. 3 ff.), frag. 80 (264. 22); Zosimus, v. 20. 1, 21. 5; Philostorgius, xi. 8 (139. 12, ed. Bidez); cf. Suidas, s.v. Φράβιθος. Contrast the case of Generidus in Zosimus, v. 46. 2–5.
[3] Amm. Marc., xvi. 12. 25.

105   I

century, was a convert to Judaism, married a Jewish wife called Sarah, and is known to us from the inscription on his tombstone.[1] But there is neither evidence nor likelihood that Fravitta's rival Eriulf, the leader of the anti-Roman faction after the battle of Adrianople, became a Christian. He was a pagan, but he subscribed to the old Gothic paganism, and that is one reason—his anti-Roman policies being the other—why Eunapius uses very different language of Eriulf from that which he uses of Fravitta.

It would seem, then, that several, if not most, of those optimates who were won over politically by Theodosius in the years following Adrianople began to accept some form of Roman religion at the same time as they entered Roman military service. Eunapius seems to suggest that some of these Gothic leaders were insincere in their new religious professions: their change of heart was designed simply to secure them political power.[2] As for the bulk of the Visigoths who stayed in Moesia until 395 and did not go off to join Theodosius, there is reason to think, as we have seen, that these became a Christian people in the years 382–95. There is explicit evidence that within this period the Christians included some of the highest members of society, for it was now that the Christian 'queen' Gaatha and her son Arimerius and her daughter Dulcilla made their fleeting appearance in history.[3] But the movement towards Christianity did not fail to call forth resistance from some of the tribesmen, though doubtless from a steadily decreasing number as the years went by and the old conditions crumbled away. Even in the late

[1] O. Fiebiger, *Inschriftensammlung*, Zweite Folge (Vienna, 1944), no. 22.
[2] Eunapius, frag. 60 (252. 23 ff.), where the word διακράτησις is difficult.
[3] Delehaye, 279. See Appendix ii.

eighties or the early nineties the friendship of Gaatha was unable to save Wella, a layman, from being stoned to death for accepting the new religion (p. 159 below). But the attack on Wella is the last violent outbreak of militant paganism inside Visigothic society of which information has reached us.

The conversion took place when the Visigoths were living in close association with the Roman inhabitants of Moesia. Since the optimates were now becoming landowners, their social interests were approximating more and more closely to the interests of the Roman landowners around them. The tribal religion had decayed with the decay of the tribes themselves; and hence, living as they were in a Roman environment, the Visigothic leaders were accepting the outlook of the Roman propertied classes whose social position they hoped to reproduce in their own society. And this was true even when their political submission to the Roman rulers was far from complete. In a word, that the Visigoths should have been converted to Christianity in these circumstances and precisely at this date is not wholly incomprehensible.

But now we come to a harder question: why did they accept Arianism rather than Catholicism? Or, to put the question more precisely, when Audianism, Catholicism, and Arianism had all three gained a footing among them, why was it that Arianism triumphed and the other two practically disappeared? To believe with some ancient writers that they embraced Arianism because Valens was an Arian is difficult, for, apart from other considerations, they were still mostly pagans when Valens died in 378. Nor can we well argue that it was Ulfila's reputation and prestige which won them over, for Ulfila's influence, so far as we know, was confined to the Christian communities: there is no evidence to suggest that he could have swayed 'the megistanes throughout Gothia' on any major issue. Again, it was held in the Roman world that the Visigoths did not understand the difference between Arianism and Catholicism and so had adopted the former owing to the 'simplicity' of their hearts.[1] This may well have been true in so far as the masses of the Visigoths were concerned: we cannot suppose that the average warrior had made a study of recent Greek Christology. But that is scarcely the point. It cannot be argued that the difference between Arianism and orthodoxy was obscure to Ulfila, or to his successor Selenas, or to Fretela and Sunnia, who discussed with St. Jerome the meaning of 178 passages of the Psalms,[2] or to the author of the Gothic Commentary on St. John's Gospel, or to the revisers of Ulfila's translation of the Bible, who are sometimes thought to have altered the Gothic in one or two places in order to lend support to the tenets of Arius.[3] In fact, there was late in the fourth century and early in the fifth a number of educated Visigoths who doubtless played a decisive part in the conversion of their countrymen to Arianism and who knew very well what they were doing. But why were they able to convince the optimates that Arianism was the true doctrine?

[1] Socrates, iv. 33. 9; cf. Procopius, *BG* viii. 4. 11; Jordanes, *Get.* xxv. 132 'rudibus et ignaris'. Sozomen, vi. 37. 8, uses ἀπερισκέπτως of Ulfila himself.
[2] See pp. 138 ff., below.
[3] At I Corinthians xv. 25 ff.; cf. G. W. S. Friedrichsen, *The Gothic Version of the Epistles* (Oxford, 1939), 233, 236 ff., and at Philippians, ii. 6, on which see (in English) *Edinburgh Review*, cxlvi (October, 1877), 376. But the Arian bias of the passage is denied by F. Jostes, *Beiträge*, xxii (1897), 186 n. 1; F. Kauffmann, 'Der Arianismus des Wulfila', *Zeitschrift für deutsche Philologie*, xxx (1898), 93–112, 96. See the notes ad loc. by E. Bernardt, *Vulfila* (Halle, 1875), 511, cf. xxx, and W. Streitberg, *Die gotische Bibel*, i. 370.

I must admit that in the total absence of Visigothic documents bearing on this question, I can give no answer. At first sight one or two lines of enquiry might seem likely to be fruitful. Thus, the Arian *Trinité hiérarchisée* (as Zeiller calls it),[1] a Godhead wherein, as the end of Ulfila's creed shows, the Holy Spirit was subject and obedient in all things to the Son, and the Son subject and obedient in all things to the Father, would accurately reflect the position which the confederate chieftain, rapidly strengthening his position in society, hoped soon to win for himself over against his followers. Such a picture would also be readily comprehensible and acceptable to the tribesmen, for 'an anthropomorphic conception of the deity would recommend itself . . . as more nearly related to their own conception, wherein the full deity was only a step beyond the demi-god, and removed from the hero more by antiquity than by omnipotence, infinity, or incomprehensibility'.[2] Again, it has been pointed out that the strict hierarchy existing within the Arian Trinity and the unqualified obedience of the lower members of it to the higher would reflect precisely the conditions of the fully developed *comitatus* ('retinue'), which existed among the fourth-century Visigoths.[3] But these are speculations, and, since there is no evidence whatever on which to base a discussion, it is hardly profitable to follow them up. Another consideration,

[1] Zeiller, op. cit. 517. See also Scott, op. cit. (on p. xiv n. 1 above), 210.
[2] Scott, op. cit. 78, cf. 109. Hence Audius' success in winning converts will not have been handicapped by his strong tendency to anthropomorphism. He stressed Genesis, ii. 26, and concluded that God has eyes and ears, works with his hands, sits down, and so on: Epiphanius, 234. 11. Note also H. Lother, *Die Christusauffassung der Germanen* (Gütersloh, 1937), 17 ff.
[3] A. Helfferich, *Der westgotische Arianismus und die spanische Ketzergeschichte* (Berlin, 1860), 22 f. Cf. the Old Saxon conception of Christ discussed by H. Gossler, *Zeitschrift für deutsche Philologie*, lix (1935), 1–52.

however, will almost certainly have had an effect on the Visigothic optimates. By accepting Catholicism they could scarcely have failed before very long to have been absorbed into the organization of the Universal Church, which in Theodosius' reign they would not all have cared to do, nor, if they had, would their followers have been likely to acquiesce in their action. As Catholics they would unquestionably have lost something of their freedom of organization. Their priests would have been liable to take their instructions from an authority outside the people, who at this date would scarcely have submitted to any form of government which was directed by Romans. Now, Arianism was not a centralized or interprovincial organization: it remained a number of essentially separate, local, and independent churches and hence was more suited organizationally to a people who wished to preserve their social identity inside the Roman Empire.

3. Ecclesiastical Organization

For some years after the first Christian war-prisoners had been carried off by the Goths in the middle of the third century, they can scarcely have had any ecclesiastical organization at all; and we do not know how such an organization came into existence and how it grew. We have seen reason to believe that some form of organization or at least of communication was in existence by 341 (p. xvii above).

Such organization as we find in Ulfila's day among Arians and Catholics alike in Gothia was based on the hierarchical Roman practice. There was a bishop called Godda, who was apparently a Catholic and who certainly lived in Ulfila's time (pp. 161 ff. below). As for the Arians, Ulfila appears to have been their temporal as well as their spiritual leader at Nicopolis. A fifth-century writer says that his power equalled that of the most absolute monarch,[1] and, although this writer's authority is in general weak, his opinion on this point would seem to be confirmed by the hold which Ulfila's successor Selenas is known to have exercised over the Gothic soldiers in Constantinople at the end of the fourth century.[2] Certainly, Ulfila, like Selenas after him, was the sole spiritual leader of his people, their only bishop: he had no clerical colleagues of equal standing with himself (p. 163 below). What we find at Nicopolis, then, is a completely separate, self-contained, and self-governing unit. We find a spiritual leadership which seems to have been combined with temporal autocracy, a spiritual community standing altogether outside the structure of the Imperial Church. This is the organization of a society in which the tribal system plays no part.

When Ulfila was living at Nicopolis his authority may have extended nominally beyond the Roman frontier into Gothia; but if so, there is no evidence that he was ever able to exercise it there in person after his flight into the Empire in 347–8. The local Arian communities in Gothia were led by presbyters, and the community whose church was burned in the persecution of 369–72 included two priests, Wereca and Batwins, both of them married and both of them the fathers of families.[3]

---

[1] Theodoret, *HE* iv. 27. In Jordanes, *Get.* li. 267, *primas* may indicate only ecclesiastical authority; but A. Lippold, P.-W. ix. A i. 517, may be right in supposing that it means temporal power.

[2] Sozomen, vii. 17. 11 f. See p. 137 below.

[3] Achelis, art. cit., 325. In the Gothic Calendar *papa = presbyter*, not 'bishop': M. H. Jellinek, 'Ahd. *phaffo*—got. *papa*', *ZfdA*, lxix (1932), 143 f. The *presbyterion* mentioned in the *Passio S. Sabae*, 221. 18, is irrelevant since it lay in the Roman province of Scythia: G. Pfeilschifter, *Festgabe Alois Knöpfler* (Munich, 1907), 203.

Now, St. Patrick during his mission to Ireland appears to have consecrated very few bishops. It is thought that he usually put his churches in the charge of priests and deacons; and many of these, like most of his bishops, are said to have been Britons or Gauls, though some Irishmen converted in the early years of the mission were considered, it seems, to be sufficiently mature as Christians to be consecrated as bishops towards the end of the mission.[1] It would have been ill-advised of Ulfila to import many Roman clerics into Gothia and to consecrate them there, for the bulk of the Visigoths whom he proposed to convert must have been very hostile to the Romans after their tragic losses in their war with Constantine in 332; and they must have been even more hostile after the Romans' brutal treatment of them in 376 (p. 22 above). Nor would it have been good tactics to elevate many of the descendants of Roman war-prisoners, for in addition to being Roman their social status in Visigothic society cannot have been high. But the number of Visigoths capable of holding episcopal office would not have been large in the opinion of so meticulous and so enormously learned a scholar as Ulfila. Therefore, even if he had wished to multiply sees in Gothia he would probably not have found it easy to discover many clerics eligible for the posts. And moreover, the difficulties of setting up a series of bishoprics in a land where there were few or no cities and where society was organized on a tribal basis were enormous, as the Celts of Ireland were to learn later on.[2] Accordingly, Ulfila appears to have gone

[1] J. L. Gough Meissner *apud* W. A. Phillips, *History of the Church of Ireland* (Oxford, 1933), i. 120 ff.
[2] In Ireland (where the Church differed, however, from the Gothic Church in the fifth century in having little contact with the Roman world) bishoprics had in many cases to be made conterminous with

further than Patrick and to have placed all his churches in the charge of priests and deacons. In other words, the Visigothic bishop, like the pagan Burgundian *sinistus*, had won a position of unique authority and security in his society which the confederate chiefs may well have envied.[1]

As for the main body of the Visigoths who settled in Moesia in 382 and after 395 travelled to Italy, Gaul, and Spain, the Christians among them formed a unit as self-contained and as distinct from its environment as the little colony at Nicopolis. Just as the Visigoths as a whole maintained their own customs, political organization, and language distinct from those of the Roman populations through whose midst they passed, so also the Visigothic Christians maintained their own ecclesiastical organization in isolation from that of the Universal Church. We catch glimpses of them as they travelled through the world, worshipping in tents or on wagons as they and their fathers had done north of the Danube in the days of Athanaric.[2] Constantly on the move as they were, it would have been impossible to attach them to the territorial divisions and subdivisions of the Roman Church, even if they had been willing to be incorporated and absorbed.

There is no record of how they appointed their bishop and their other priests. According to one view, 'it would have meant a complete and voluntary renunciation of one of the optimates' most important rights, on which their authority rested to a considerable

tribal lands, a fact which had strange results on the ecclesiastical organization there: J. B. Bury, *The Life of St. Patrick* (London, 1905), 179–82, 375–9.

[1] See p. 58 above.

[2] Jerome, *Ep.* cvii. 2; Ambrose, *Ep.* xx. 12 (Migne, *PL* xvi. 1039); Sozomen, vi. 37. 14 f.

extent, if they had foregone all influence on the
organization of the new religion, on the office of the
priesthood, and particularly on the selection and
nomination to it'.[1] There is little reason, of course, for
supposing that barbarian heretics would have considered themselves bound by canon 13 of the Council
of Laodicea, which laid it down that the 'multitudes'
should not be allowed to make the choice of those who
were to be appointed to the priestly office.[2] But Ulfila
had been appointed by Eusebius of Nicomedia, and
about the year 400 the Catholic bishop of the Crimean
Ostrogoths was appointed by the Patriarch of Constantinople. The procedure of these Ostrogoths is
known; for when their bishop Unila, who had been
consecrated by John Chrysostom, died in 404, the local
chief sent a deacon named Moduarius to Constantinople
to announce the vacancy and to request the appointment of a successor to Unila.[3] This, of course, does not
necessarily throw light on the practice of the Arian
Visigoths. But it is clear that there was no tradition of a
popularly elected prelate among the Gothic Christians
as a whole. And yet we must suppose that the people
did indeed have some voice in making the appointments,
for they still had some say in Spain in the seventh
century; and a growth of democratic rights in the

[1] H. von Schubert, *Staat und Kirche in den arianischen Königreichen*
(Munich and Berlin, 1912), 70, and the whole passage, 65 ff. Note that
the Arian Sunna is explicitly stated to have been appointed bishop of
Mérida by king Leovigild: *Vitas SS. Patrum Emeretensium*, v. 5. 2 (ed. J. N.
Garvin, Washington, 1946).

[2] On the election of bishops see G. E. M. de Ste. Croix, *British Journal
of Sociology*, v (1954), 36. The people of Grenoble elected a priest shortly
after 516 to the great annoyance of the bishop: Avitus, *Ep.* lxxv.

[3] John Chrysostom, *Ep.* xiv. (For another Ostrogoth called Unila see
Procopius, *BG* v. 16. 5.) In 548–9 the Trapezite Goths on the death of
their bishop sent four envoys to Justinian asking him to give them
another bishop: ibid., viii. 4. 12, which passage suggests that this was an
innovation in the mid-sixth century.

meantime may be ruled out as inconceivable. The matter was raised at the provincial synod of the province of Tarraconensis held at Barcelona in 599 in the reign of the first Catholic Visigothic king Reccared (586–601). It was there enacted that the practice was to be as follows: two or three men of suitable character, who had duly gone through the ecclesiastical grades, were to be selected by the clergy and people, and their names were to be submitted to the metropolitan and his fellow-bishops, whose choice was to be final. The fact that the people were given some say in the selection was not a mere local custom restricted to Tarraconensis; for in 633 at the Fourth Council of Toledo, which was national and not provincial, it was enacted that no one could become a bishop whom the clergy and people of his own city had not chosen.[1] It is not unreasonable to suppose that this was a right of the people which the authorities had not been able to crush even in the seventh century.

4. Ulfila's Achievement

Apart from his Bible Ulfila published much; but many of his books seem to have been devoted to the question of the difference between the Father's divinity and the Son's. They were in some cases written in no very amicable tone—all who did not accept the creed of Rimini (p. xix above), Homoousians and Homoiousians alike, were dismissed without compunction as nothing less than Antichrists.[2] But our ignorance might be less

[1] Mansi, x, 482 f., 625.
[2] Auxentius, 64. 1, 9 ff. K. K. Klein, *ZfdA*, lxxxiv (1952), 110 ff., supposes that the polemical tone of this passage is due to Auxentius and not to Ulfila himself, because it 'entspricht der Geistesart des Meisters und auch dessen Haltung an seinem Lebensabend in keiner Weise'. But how do we know that?

profound if we still possessed the tracts and commentaries which he published in Greek, Latin, and Gothic; for his Gothic books were designed in some cases not for the defence of Arianism but for the edification of his hearers.[1] Some of these works may have perished when king Reccared was converted to Catholicism in Spain in 589, for he ordered all Arian books to be surrendered and burned,[2] and his orders were carried out to such effect that not a single Gothic text has survived in Spain. Ulfila's successor Selenas, son of a Gothic father and a Phrygian mother, was bilingual in Gothic and Greek, and he preached in both languages, but there is no record that he published in either.[3] The fact, however, that Ulfila published in Gothic at all shows that a number of Visigoths were now literate in their own language and in their new alphabet; but by 'publication' we can hardly mean much more than that Ulfila distributed some of his writings among the narrow circle of his fellow-clerics for their private study and edification. But before anyone could read them at all, some knowledge of the new alphabet in which they were written must have been propagated by its inventor. As part of his monumental labours Ulfila must have spent time in 'writing alphabets' for those who proposed to study and preach from the new translation of the Bible, just as Patrick in Ireland 'wrote abgatoriae' for some of *his* disciples.[4] But whereas in Patrick's case this was the first step in teaching Latin to his converts, in the case of Ulfila it was the first step

---

[1] Auxentius, 74. 43.   [2] See p. 155 f. below.
[3] Socrates, v. 23. 8; Sozomen, vii. 17. 12.
[4] Tírachán, vi. xiii, xxxiii, xxxvii, xliii, xlv, xlvii = respectively Rolls ed., 304. 3, 308. 13, 320. 28, 322. 15, 326. 29, 327. 20, 328. 28. Even though Tírachán's specific examples may be unhistorical, we cannot doubt the general fact that Patrick frequently 'wrote alphabets'.

in teaching not only converts but also those who were already Christian to write their own language.

When Patrick went to Ireland he brought with him a Latin Bible, and he did not produce any translation of it into Irish. He educated his priests in the Latin tradition, and hence the Irish clergy had access to the whole body of Western Christian literature. This is one reason why they were so skilled in later centuries at working out their own individual course of development, and why it came about that Ireland was inhabited by scholars as well as by saints. It may be wondered, therefore, whether Ulfila was wise from his own point of view in the conditions of the fourth century in bringing to the Germanic peoples a Gothic Bible rather than a Greek or Latin one. No characteristic of Germanic Arian theology is more marked than its aridity, its refusal to speculate, its pedestrian earthbound barrenness and lack of originality. One reason for its poverty may be that by providing a Gothic Bible and liturgy Ulfila cut off the Germanic clergy to some extent from the riches of Greek theology. Even though many of them must have known either Greek or Latin, and even though their own literature (which is not known to have been extensive) included translations, they lived in some isolation from the great theological movements of the outside world. On the other hand, a Latin Bible and liturgy would perhaps have identified the new religion so closely with the Romans as to repel Goths who might otherwise have been sympathetic to it.

However that may be, Ulfila's activities as a teacher were not directed only at Goths. His Greek and Latin publications must have been directed at the inhabitants of the Roman provinces. When he settled in the Empire he made himself so far acceptable to well-to-do Arian

Romans that they were willing to entrust their sons to his care and tuition. One of these pupils afterwards wrote: 'I cannot praise him as I ought, and I do not dare to pass him by in complete silence, for to him above all others I am debtor in as much as he laboured more abundantly in me, having in my earliest days taken me from my parents to be his pupil and taught me sacred letters and made the truth clear to me. And through the mercy of God and the grace of Christ he educated me both carnally and spiritually as his own son in the faith.'[1]

What comment are we to make on the greatness of Ulfila if we grant that the mass of the Visigoths were still pagan when he died? The invention of the alphabet and the translation of the Bible in the conditions of the fourth century were beyond doubt a colossal achievement. This is true even if the translation was a collective work carried out by a group of translators working under his direction; for the finished product bears the stamp of one man's methods and technique in spite of the alterations which were introduced into the text after Ulfila was dead.[2] But the greatness of the translation must not be allowed to overshadow the other spheres of his activity. He must have left behind him an active and able school of clerics who grasped the opportunity which the course of history was to offer them in Theodosius' reign. They must have gone among the optimates in Moesia in 382–95 so as to explain the tenets of Arian Christianity and to instruct them in the faith. That such men were available was due to the solid groundwork of Ulfila, though not a single one of

---

[1] Auxentius, 75. 1 ff.
[2] On the question of the multiple authorship of the Gothic Bible see Friedrichsen, op. cit. (on p. 108, n. 3 above), 257 ff.

them is known by name.[1] And men of the calibre of
Auxentius, Maximinus, and Selenas also show how
effective was the schooling of the great bishop.[2] If
Ulfila himself was not the direct cause of the conversion
of 382–95, yet that conversion would scarcely have been
achieved, at any rate in the form which it actually took,
had it not been for his preliminary work.

5. The Bishop Maximinus

Lack of evidence makes it practically impossible to
penetrate into the thought-world of the Visigoths of
Ulfila's time. We have already quoted the words of
Auxentius, bishop of Durostorum, on his indebtedness
to his master; but Auxentius' works can give us but
little help in this connexion, for, although he was a pupil
of Ulfila, it is almost certain that he was not a Goth. We
have from his pen a priceless document, a letter which
is thought to have been written in Constantinople in
381 or a year or two later and perhaps to have been
addressed to the Arians of Dacia and Moesia.[3] It is our
chief source of information about the life of Ulfila, but
nowhere does it mention that Ulfila had translated
the Bible into the language of a horde of barbarians. In

---

[1] Auxentius, 75. 6 f., 11 f.: 'ut regeret et corrigeret, doceret et aedifi-
caret gentem Gothorum, quod et deo volente et Cristo aucsiliante per
ministerium ipsius admirabiliter est adinpletus', etc.

[2] The education of a native clergy is, of course, an old element in the
technique of missionaries: see e.g. Bede, *de Templo Salomonis* ii (*Opera*,
viii. 267, ed. Giles); Gregory the Great, *Ep.* vi. 10. But there is no more
sympathy for the barbarians in the works of Roman Arians than in those
of Roman Catholics: see *Opus Imperfectum in Matthaeum*, Homily i and
xxxv (Migne, *PG* lvi. 626, 824, cf. 864).

[3] So F. Kauffmann, *Aus der Schule des Wulfila* (Strasbourg, 1899), lix,
n. 3; cf. Zeiller, op. cit. 497, n. 3; Klein, art. cit. 146–9. The identifi-
cation of this Auxentius with Auxentius *alias* Mercurinus has never been
proved: the arguments of K. K. Klein, *Beiträge*, lxxv (1953), 165–91,
show no more than that both men were associated with 'Scythia' and
that they held similar views on a number of questions.

119

Auxentius' eyes Ulfila was a member of the Christian Church, an Arian controversialist, an inhabitant of the Roman Empire winning converts for the Roman faith, rather than a Goth and the Apostle of the Goths.[1] But perhaps we can form an idea of the extent to which some of the Gothic Christians assimilated the outlook of the Roman educated classes if we examine the works of the Arian bishop Maximinus, who is sometimes said to have been himself a Goth and who certainly associated closely with Goths and preached to them and whose works were read and studied by Goths.

He was born about 359, and towards end of his career was attached to the 'Roman' army, largely consisting of Goths, which Count Sigisvult led to Africa in 428.[2] All his surviving works, except the *Dissertation against Ambrose*, are preserved in a manuscript of the early sixth century;[3] and their first editor, the eighteenth-century scholar B. Bruni (1784), ascribed them to Maximus, the famous Catholic bishop of Turin in the middle of the fifth century. This ascription was accepted with little or no hesitation by eminent scholars,[4] until in 1922 the true authorship was discovered.[5] This in itself is an illuminating

---

[1] Kauffmann, op. cit., lix.

[2] Prosper, 1294, cf. J. L. M. de Lepper, *De Rebus Gestis Bonifatii* (Breda, 1941), 60–63, and his index s.v. 'Sigisvultus'. It is doubtful whether he was the Maximinus who accompanied Geiseric to Sicily in 440. On his career see Kauffmann, op. cit., liv ff.

[3] On the date of the Codex Verona li (49) see E. A. Lowe, *Classical Quarterly*, xix (1925), 202 f.

[4] See e.g. C. H. Turner, *JTS*, xvii (1916), 235, who, however, acknowledged Capelle's 'startling discovery', ibid., xxiv (1923), 76. Capelle's work, cited in the next note, is described by A. Wilmart, *Revue biblique*, xxxvi (1927), 61, as constituting 'une des plus importantes découvertes des dernières années dans le champ de l'ancienne littérature latine'.

[5] By D. B. Capelle, *RB*, xxxiv (1922), 81–108; ibid., xl (1928), 49–86, the latter article containing the text of 23 homilies on the Gospel. For the text of other works of Maximinus see ibid., xxxviii (1926), 5–15; C. H.

phenomenon. Maximinus, Arian though he was, had so
far accommodated his outlook to that of the Catholics
that most of his works were all but indistinguishable
from theirs. But in fact he subscribed to the creed of
Rimini,[1] and the Arian element does indeed come out
in one or two of his works.[2] It is not at all certain that
his sermons were delivered exclusively to Roman
congregations,[3] and they indicate strikingly the degree
to which the Goths in his congregations had cut themselves off from their fellow-tribesmen and had allowed
themselves to be absorbed into the society of their
hereditary enemies. Yet Maximinus' sermons were
popular reading with the Goths. A sixth-century
Ostrogoth read our manuscript of the Homilies shortly
after it was written and noted in the margin in Gothic
the subject-matter of each Homily. A dozen of his notes,
written in the Gothic script, can still be read, although
some of them were partially erased by a later orthodox
owner of the manuscript. He had Ulfila's text of the
Bible beside him as he wrote, and he preserves a few
scraps of it (from St. Luke's Gospel) which are otherwise lost.[4]

Turner and A. Spagnolo, *JTS*, xiii (1912), 19–28; xvi (1915), 161–76,
314–22; xvii (1916), 225–35, 321–37; xx (1919), 289–310.
[1] Augustine, *Coll. cum Maximino* (Migne, *PL* xlii. 710 f.); cf. F.
Kauffmann, *Zeitschrift für deutsche Philologie*, xxx (1898), 108–110;
Capelle, art. cit. (1922), 92–4.
[2] Ibid., 90. For Maximinus' Arianism see esp. the *Dissertatio* and the
sermon printed in *JTS* (1912). Unhappily, that sermon appears to be
incomplete: it may originally have been a *Contra Haereticos*, forming with
the *Contra Iudaeos* and the *Contra Paganos* the third treatise of a trilogy.
But immediately before it in the manuscript at least 11 leaves have been
removed by some orthodox reader of about the seventh century:
Turner, ibid., xxiv (1923), 78.
[3] Friedrichsen, op. cit. 263, 'We are surely not bound to conclude that
these sermons were written exclusively for Romans'; and it is clear that
e.g. Homily xx, printed by Capelle (1928), 70, would have more point
if it were delivered to a partly barbarian audience.
[4] Capelle (1928), 50 f.; C. von Kraus, 'Gotica Veronensia', *ZfdA*, lxvi

The content of these tracts and sermons is interesting. The tract against the Jews is a contribution to the doctrinal polemic waged between the doctors of Christianity and those of Judaism; but Maximinus' work can lay little claim to originality. In a somewhat confused manner he follows the schema traditional in Roman polemics against the Jews, and the arguments employed inside this schema are themselves for the most part traditional.[1] We do not know where or in what circumstances Maximinus composed this work or to what Jews, if any, he addressed it, so that it tells us little about him in his social context. His tract against the pagans, written later than the year 400, is directed primarily against the old Roman religion and philosophy: it has little or no reference to a barbarian people recently converted from tribal paganism. The type of argument which Maximinus employs is purely literary and could only have been fully understood by men educated in the Christian Latin tradition. Interminable citation of the Scriptures is supported by very numerous quotations from Cyprian and other Christian writers and even from Cicero and Virgil. The appeal of Maximinus' arguments is neither Gothic nor popular: he addresses himself almost entirely to educated Romans.

The sermons, too, are illuminating. They were delivered at widely different times in Maximinus' long career as a preacher—so much so indeed that even his spelling of some words seems to have changed in the interval between the writing of the earlier sermons and

(1929), 209–213; P. Gothein, 'Zu den Gotica Veronensia', ibid., lxvii (1930), 207; J. W. Marchand, 'Notes on Gothic Manuscripts', *Journal of English and Germanic Philology*, lvi (1957), 215–17.

[1] For Roman polemics against the Jews see M. Simon, *Verus Israel* (Paris, 1948), 166 ff.

that of the later.[1] A Benedictine who has edited some of them comments on Maximinus' astonishing knowledge of the text of the Scriptures,[2] his almost complete failure to draw any practical lesson from the texts, his entire lack of originality, the succession of mystical interpretations and fantastic developments, the general aridity and barrenness.[3] Throughout its history, as we have said, Germanic Arianism was characterized by a ponderous and earthbound reliance on the text of the Bible.[4] Similarly, the fragments of the so-called *Skeireins*, an anonymous Gothic commentary on St. John's Gospel, keep closely to the task of exegesis with one or two excursions into polemic against Sabellius and Marcellus; and at any rate in the eight manuscript leaves which are all of it that we possess the author, who is thought to have been contemporary with Ulfila and who was beyond question an Arian[5] and a well-read scholar, draws no lessons bearing on daily conduct and no conclusions of practical value.[6] In this respect Maximinus was typical, so far as we can judge, of Gothic

[1] Capelle (1928), 76, 82 n. 1.
[2] Cf. his words to Augustine at the beginning of the *Collatio* (Migne, *PL* xlii. 709): 'eae voces quae extra Scripturam sunt nullo casu a nobis suscipiuntur', cf. viii (col. 726), 'quod lego, credo'.
[3] Capelle (1928), 87 f. See ibid., 104, for a possible reference in Maximinus to the Gothic martyrs. Several of the works give the impression of having been written in Africa: read e.g. sermon xii in *JTS*, xvi (1915), 321, and for African influence on Maximinus' text of the Bible see Capelle (1928), 83.
[4] See Capelle's judgement, ibid., 50, on Maximinus, and that of Kauffmann, op. cit., lv f., on the *Dissertatio*.
[5] On his Arianism see Streitberg, op. cit., i. 370 (on Philippians, ii. 6).
[6] The opinion of its editor, E. Dietrich, *Die Bruchstücke der Skeireins* (Strasbourg, 1903), lxx ff., that the work is by Ulfila himself, is not cogent, though it has been thought probable by e.g. Zeiller, op. cit., 505–10. See the references in K. Helm, 'Einiges über die Skeireins', *Beiträge*, lxxx (1958), 201–7, at 204 f. For the best text of the Skeireins see W. H. Bennett, *The Gothic Commentary on the Gospel of John*, The Modern Language Association of America: Monograph Series xx (New York, 1960).

theologians. And like the author of the *Skeireins* he was no mean scholar: he had read himself into the tradition, pagan as well as Christian, of the educated Romans of his time. One of the most striking characteristics of his work is his borrowing from his predecessors. He draws on Optatus,[1] and frequently on Cyprian and even on contemporary Catholic writers like Ambrose, Hilary, and Rufinus.[2] His knowledge of Cicero, too, is such that he preserves a fragment of the *Hortensius* which is known from no other source. Virgil he has studied with admiration, and although he is not above dropping a hint that pagan books might well be burned he more than once quotes 'that outstanding poet'.[3]

Only once in his sermons does Maximinus come out of the clouds and descend to earth, and then it is for no very laudable purpose. 'He is truly the rich man of God', says he in his eighteenth Homily,[4] 'who gives to the sighing poor and not to the dancing actor. It is true that there are many wealthy bishops and priests and deacons; but he who disposes well of his riches cannot incur blame for luxury or the stain of crime or the penalty of damnation. Indeed, God wished some men to be rich precisely in order that there might be those who would give to the poor; and He made some men poor in order that they might receive the necessities of life from the rich. For God's plan is holy in all things, to

---

[1] D. B. Capelle, *RB*, xxxv (1923), 24–6, who says that this borrowing shows Optatus' sermon to have been known in Illyricum. But is not Maximinus more likely to have read it when he was himself in Africa?

[2] Turner and Spagnolo, *JTS*, xvii (1916), 234 n. 1, and throughout the critical notes to their editions. See also J. Baxter, ibid., xxi (1920), 175–7. Cyprian is also quoted in the *Dissertatio*, 68. 26 ff.; cf. Zeiller, op. cit. 487.

[3] *JTS*, xvii (1916), 322. 53, 326, 328. In Homily xviii, printed in Capelle (1928), 68, he quotes *Georgics*, i. 84–92, cf. *JTS*, xvi (1915), 175.

[4] Capelle (1928), 71 *fin.*

be reverenced in all its parts, and to be praised for ever.' So Maximinus felt himself obliged to assert that the maldistribution of wealth among the brethren was sanctioned by God. One may wonder whether *all* those who heard this sermon were convinced that the inequality of the social classes had originated as Maximinus here asserts.[1]

Even though he was not one of the company of Visigoths who marched to the West with Alaric, the works of Maximinus provide an eloquent, though extreme, witness of the extent to which Christian Goths could become Romanized in the early years of the fifth century[2] and of how quickly Christianity was made into a sanction for the new kind of society which had replaced tribalism.

The only other heretical barbarian on whose religious beliefs we have some detailed information is the Burgundian king Gundobad, who reigned in Savoy from about 480 until his death in 516. (The Burgundians were converted to Christianity *c.* 430.)[3] Most of our knowledge of the king comes from the correspondance of Alcimus Avitus, bishop of Vienne, who died in 518. Towards the beginning of his association with the bishop, Gundobad had arranged a debate on points of dogma between the Arian and Catholic bishops of his kingdom. When the debate was over, he instructed Avitus to forward in writing the arguments which had been used, as many of these had been new to him and he wished to review them in consultation with his

---

[1] For another Arian's view see *Opus Imperfectum in Matthaeum*, homily xlvi (Migne, *PL* lvi. 892). But not all Romans allowed themselves to be hoodwinked by such a naive sophistry: see e.g. the anonymous Pelagian's *Tractatus de Divitiis*, xii. 1–2, ed. C. Caspari, 48.

[2] This is the judgement of Friedrichsen, op. cit. 263.

[3] E. A. Thompson *apud* A. Momigliano (ed.), *The Conflict Between Paganism and Christianity in the Fourth Century* (Oxford, 1963), 71 f.

Arian bishops.[1] Thereafter the king sent letter after letter to Avitus asking for an exposition of passages of the Bible,[2] raising points of dogma,[3] requiring a refutation of Eutychianism,[4] and so on. Nor was Avitus the only Catholic to be favoured. Even a Catholic layman might speak up freely for his faith in the king's presence and might hope to make some impression on his audience.[5] Not only did Avitus answer the specific questions of the king, but sometimes when they had been talking together he would reproduce their discussions in writing or at any rate the main lines of their argument; and these dialogues were subsequently published.[6] The king's attitude differed little from that of Maximinus or the author of the *Skeireins*. He had a detailed knowledge of the text of the Latin Bible, though there is no evidence that he ever used Ulfila's Gothic. Eutychianism was to be refuted by the largest possible number of citations from the Bible.[7] The words of the Bible were to be interpreted literally, though when the king raised the question of whether he ought to forsake all in accordance with Matthew, xix. 21 ff., Avitus was happily able to reassure him: a higher interpretation of the passage provided an escape-clause for kings like Gundobad.[8] There was no question of original theological thought on Gundobad's part: he was as earthbound as Maximinus. It is hardly surprising that Germanic Arianism was doomed to extinction.

[1] Avitus, *Ep.* xxiii. On the date see M. Burckhardt, *Die Briefsammlung Bischofs Avitus von Vienne* (Berlin, 1938), 59. For official debates between Arian and Catholic bishops before Visigothic Arian kings see *Vitas SS. Patrum Emeretensium*, v. 5. 9 ff.; Gregory of Tours, *Hist. Franc.* ix. 15. For an example from Vandal Africa see Victor Vitensis, *Hist. Persec.* ii. 39 ff.

[2] *Epp.* vi, xxi, xxii.   [3] Ibid., ii, iii, iv, xxx.
[4] Idem, *Contra Eutych.*, init.   [5] Idem, *Epp.* liii, liv.
[6] Agobard of Lyons (769–840) in Peiper's ed. of Avitus, 2; cf. Burckhardt, op. cit., 13.
[7] Avitus, *In Eutych.*, i, init.   [8] Idem, *Ep.* vi.

6. The Conversion of the Barbarians

Before 476, when the Western Empire disappeared as a political entity, there were Christians beyond the northern Roman frontier, but they were not numerous. German mercenaries who had been converted when serving in the Imperial armies, Christian Roman prisoners who had been carried off by barbarian raiding parties, and possibly Christian traders who hawked their wares beyond the Danube, converted individual tribesmen to the Roman religion, but they did not convert entire peoples. Of professional Roman missionaries, like Patrick among the Irish, none is known to have worked among the Germans outside the frontier before the fall of the Western Empire with the insignificant exception of Audius.[1] When we ask, then, in what circumstances the major Germanic peoples were converted, we find that three propositions seem to be consistent with such evidence as exists: (i) as long as they remained outside the Roman frontiers none of the Germanic peoples (except only the Rugi in Lower Austria) became predominantly Christian before 476; (ii) all the peoples who entered the provinces before that date were converted to Christianity within a generation of their arrival in the Empire; (iii) the conversion was brought about by the activities of German and especially Gothic missionaries, not by Roman ones; but the successes of the Gothic missionaries were not won outside the Roman frontier—they were won among Germans who were already living in the Empire or astride its frontiers.[2] In other words, the

[1] See p. 82 above. Besides Ulfila notice also the Visigoths Inna, Rema, and Pinna, who worked among their countrymen: Delehaye, 215 f.
[2] These points are argued at length in Thompson, op. cit.

127

conversion to Christianity (if we exclude the Rugi)[1] is only found in association with the act of settlement in the Imperial provinces; and no case of mass settlement in the provinces is known which was not quickly followed by conversion to Christianity. Since the known examples are numerous, it is not unreasonable to think that there is no coincidence here and that the conversion was an integral and indeed inevitable part of the process of settlement in the Empire. Our conjectures about the Visigothic conversion may suggest that the transformation of the tribal optimates into a landowning aristocracy inevitably involved the adoption by them of the religion of the Roman landowners whose manner of life they intended to share or to imitate. Even in the latest days of Visigothic Spain, however, the Gothic landowners never completely merged with the Romans: they were always members of a distinct nationality. And so long as the Western Empire lasted—and in some cases even longer—the barbarians inside its frontiers kept themselves distinct from the Romans by adhering to a form of Christianity (Arianism) which was clearly marked off from the official Roman religion and was indeed persecuted by the Emperors. Moreover, when the Burgundians in 516 and the Visigoths in 589 became officially Catholic, the victory of Catholicism was regarded by many of the barbarians themselves as a defeat for the barbarian element in the population of Burgundy and Spain.

It would seem to be the case, then, that the essential factors in the conversion of any one Germanic people were (i) the existence of a decaying tribal system and hence of a decaying tribal religion; (ii) the transfer of the whole community into a Roman environment and

---

[1] For these see ibid., 76 f.

EARLY VISIGOTHIC CHRISTIANITY

the transformation of the tribal optimates into a landed gentry who reached some sort of agreement with the Roman ruling classes and who, instead of trying to overthrow the Roman society of the provinces where they settled, entered into that society to some extent and themselves became part of it; (iii) the existence of a native clergy able and eager to expound the doctrines of Arianism, though without the two preceding conditions the existence of these men would probably have been of little historical significance. That these men existed and were ready to begin their work among each people as it arrived in the Empire is a great achievement of Ulfila and his school.

Whether or not these considerations are near the mark, a word on method may not be out of place. A study of such Roman missionaries as are known to have preached to the invaders who were moving about the provinces—such men as Amantius, Nicetas of Remesiana, and others[1]—will do little in itself to explain why the Germanic peoples turned to Christianity. The evidence about the work of these men is negligible. The conversion must not be studied simply or mainly as an episode in the life of the individual missionary but as an episode in the general history of the converted people. The essential fact is not the missionary's eloquence or his diplomatic skill or his high morality or his strength of character, important though these may be. We know much about all these qualities, for example, in the case of Otto of Bamberg at a later date, and yet in themselves they tell us little about the basic reasons for the conversion of the Slavs of Pomerania. We know something about these qualities in the case of St. Patrick; yet few would claim to understand the conversion of the Irish.

[1] Ibid., 64–8.

129

We have a magnificent account of St. Ansgar's missionary work in the first half of the ninth century; but how
can it help us to understand the conversion of the
Danes or the Swedes, who in fact remained pagan for
a century or two after Ansgar's death and even forgot
that Ansgar had ever existed?[1] But in the case of Ulfila
we know practically nothing. How then can it be
supposed that the study of Ulfila's character, career,
and creed will explain the conversion of the Visigoths,
which seems to have taken place after he was dead?
The point is very clear in the case of the Saxons. In
spite of all our knowledge of the way in which St.
Boniface applied himself to the work of converting
them, the fact remains that his career was a failure in
the end, and the information given in his *Vitae* and in
his correspondance is of little direct value for understanding the conversion. (It is of much indirect value,
of course, for the incidental statements in these documents help us to reconstruct the social history of the
Saxons.) The Saxons were in fact converted many years
after Boniface's death in 754. For no less than thirty-
three years (772–804) the Franks fought them, burning
and butchering until they destroyed Saxon society in
the form in which it had existed hitherto, and hence—
since a tribal religion cannot be abstracted from the
tribes themselves or have any existence independently
of them—they destroyed or at least mutilated the Saxon
religion, too. They also succeeded in driving a wedge
between the Saxon tribal nobility and the mass of the
Saxons; and they so transformed Saxon society as to
convert into a ruling class those of the Saxon optimates
who were willing to accept Christianity: they sometimes
even went so far as to appoint such men to important

[1] L. Bril, *Revue d'histoire ecclésiastique*, xii (1911), 34–7.

Frankish offices. This new ruling class depended for the maintenance of its social position on the Frankish authorities, who would support them only if they were Christian. Christianity was one of the instruments by means of which the Franks maintained their rule over the defeated people.[1] Here is a contemporary poet's cynical and candid comment on the process:

> Nam se quisquis commiserat eius
> egregiae fidei ritus spernendo profanos
> hunc opibus ditans ornabat honoribus amplis.
> copia pauperibus Saxonibus agnita primum
> tunc fuerat rerum, quas Gallia fert opulenta,
> praedia praestiterat cum rex compluribus illic,
> ex quibus acciperent preciosae tegmina vestis,
> argenti cumulos dulcisque fluenta Liei.
> his ubi primores donis illexerat omnes
> subiectos sibimet reliquos obtriverat armis.[2]

The poet would have explained almost the whole process if he had thought of telling us how it came about that at this time, unlike former times, all the *primores* were willing to accept the fine clothes, the silver, and the wine of France. At all events, the tactics described by the poet succeeded where the great St. Boniface had failed.

It would appear, then, that the only hopeful method of reaching a comparatively satisfactory explanation is to regard the conversion as the outcome of a general change in the social relationships of the Visigoths, and hence to study the social development of the people as a

---

[1] R. E. Sullivan, 'The Carolingian Missionary and the Pagan', *Speculum*, xxviii (1953), 704–40, esp. 722 ff. (who does not, however, show the connexion between the Saxon 'factions', which he mentions, and the destruction of Saxon tribalism); F. Philippi, *Historische Zeit-schrift*, xxxix (1924), 189–232.
[2] Poeta Saxo, iv. 125–34 (*MGH., Poetae Lat. Aevi Carolini*, iv. 49).

whole and to account for the conversion in terms of that study. Considering the state of our evidence, an attempt to study the psychology of the individual missionaries or of the individual converts is not likely to be fruitful, least of all in the case of Ulfila and the Visigoths.

CHAPTER SIX

AFTER ULFILA

SURPRISINGLY little is known of the Arianism or the Arian Church organization of the Visigoths during the fifth century, when they lived in southern Gaul. But fortunately some matters have been recorded about the Goths living in Constantinople in the decades which followed immediately on Ulfila's death. I shall discuss in turn (i) John Chrysostom's efforts to convert the Arian Goths to Catholicism; (ii) the Psathyrians; (iii) the letter of St. Jerome to Sunnia and Fretela; and (iv) the later history of Ulfila's Gothic text of the Bible.

1. John Chrysostom and the Goths

John Chrysostom tried to counteract the Arianism of the Goths in Constantinople by setting aside for them a church to be used for Catholic services; and he appointed priests, deacons, and readers, who knew the Gothic language, to speak to them and expound the tenets of Nicaea. He often went there himself and preached through an interpreter, and incited others to do the same. It is said that he made many converts; but in fact the bulk of the Goths in the eastern capital were still Arian long after he was dead.[1] It is fortunate that one of the sermons still survives which John preached in 399 'in the church beside the church of Paul'. (The Paul to whom this church was dedicated, by the way, was not the apostle Paul, though this was often thought in the fifth century to be the case: it was the Paul who

---

[1] Theodoret, *Hist. Eccles.* v. 30.

had been bishop of Constantinople towards the end of the reign of Constantine the Great.)[1] The title of the sermon tells us that the preacher spoke 'after Goths had read and a Gothic presbyter had preached'.[2] Presumably they had spoken in Gothic rather than in Greek, though the title of the sermon does not make that point explicitly. In the course of his address John speaks defensively of his 'causing barbarians to rise up in the midst and speak', a procedure, he says, which no one must consider to be a disgrace.[3] On the contrary, it is a matter for congratulation to have seen 'the most barbarous of all men [a somewhat unflattering description of members of his congregation] standing along with the sheep of the Church with a common pasture and one fold and the same table set before all alike'.[4] Was not Abraham, the earliest ancestor of the Church and the Synagogue,—was not Moses himself a 'barbarian from the midst of Persia'? Did not Jesus Christ on his arrival in the world call barbarians before all other men—for the Magi, too, were Persians? Throughout the sermon John makes his points with the aid of a number of Scriptural quotations which the barbarians in his audience may not have found easy to identify. And at one point their darkness was not illumined by

[1] P. xvi above; Sozomen, vii. 10. 4. For Paul in this connexion see Socrates, v. 9. 2; Sozomen, loc. cit. P. Batiffol, 'De quelques homélies de S. Jean Chrysostome et de la version gothique des écritures', *Revue biblique*, viii (1899), 566–72, at 568, observes that 'the church of the Goths' in Constantinople, mentioned by Socrates, vi. 6. 28, must have been Catholic, as John had successfully opposed Gainas' demand for an Arian church inside the walls. This Catholic church was destroyed on 12 July 400 during the rising against Gainas, *Chron. Pasch.*, s.a. 400.

[2] John Chrysostom, *Homilia habita postquam Gothus*, etc. (Migne, *PG* lxiii. 499–510), with Batiffol, art. cit. John brushes aside the Arian controversy: καὶ γὰρ ἐν τῇ μήτρᾳ ὢν τῇ παρθενικῇ, μετὰ τοῦ Πατρὸς ἦν, τὸ δὲ πῶς μὴ ζήτει μηδὲ εὐθύνας ἀπαίτει. ὅταν γὰρ ὁ Θεὸς ἐργάζηται, πίστεως χρεία μόνης καὶ συγκαταθέσεως καὶ ὁμολογίας.

[3] Col. 501.   [4] Col. 502.

John's explicit refusal to explain the reference in one of his quotations: 'I am able to tell you', he says, 'but in order that you may not learn everything from me, do you yourselves meditate and lie awake and search the treasures of the Holy Writ, find the passage in the prophet, and you will know who the king was, and of what nation, and when he lived.' (The reference, in fact, is to Isaiah, xiv. 12.) Then he quotes Proverbs, ix. 9 'Give instruction to a wise man, and he will be yet wiser'.[1] Most of the sermon is devoted to the part which barbarians, and particularly the Magi, have played in the growth of Christianity; and the theme is intended to flatter his audience and make them feel proud to be Christian. But towards the end of the sermon the theme suddenly changes, and John attacks the belief that all human action is governed and controlled by Fate or Necessity. We have no means of saying what was the relevance of this to his Gothic hearers. Whether a belief in some kind of Fate had been part of the pagan religion which they had so recently abandoned, or whether the argument was directed at some of John's own opponents in the Eastern capital, is difficult to tell.

2. The Psathyrians

Soon after the year 386 an illuminating series of events took place in Constantinople. The Arian Christians there and elsewhere split over an issue which might be called (to use a moderate expression) an academic one, though in fact it was very far from being a new one. In the opinion of the Arians the Father had begotten the Son in time, and the Son did not exist from all eternity (p. xxi above): was God, then, eternally

[1] Col. 506.

the 'Father', or was it inexact to speak of Him as 'Father' when referring to the time when the Son was not yet in existence? The point had been discussed by Arius himself in his *Thalia* (to the delight of Athanasius, who did not fail to make use of the ammunition thus supplied to him).[1] Different answers had been given to the problem;[2] and when even a Byzantine ecclesiastical historian says that the question was something of a quibble,[3] we may not be reluctant to agree with him. Yet this puzzle divided the Arians of Constantinople for more than thirty years at the end of the fourth century and the beginning of the fifth, and it divided the Arians of other cities for even longer.

After the death of Demophilus (p. xx above) in 386, the Arians of the capital appointed one Marinus as their bishop, but then expelled him and summoned Dorotheus, Arian bishop of Antioch, to take his place. Dorotheus declared that since the Word, according to the Arians, was not begotten by God but had been constituted out of nothing, God had not always been the 'Father'. Marinus, on the other hand, piqued at his displacement by Dorotheus, took him up on this point, and maintained that God *had* been the Father even when the Son did not yet exist. The split was complete. Dorotheus' party held on to the Arian meeting-places: Marinus and his followers held separate meetings in houses of their own. The latter sect were commonly called the 'Psathyrians' because one of their warmer-headed supporters, a Syrian named Theoctistus, was a *psathyropoles*, a seller of some kind of crumbly cakes. The Psathyrians next proceeded to subdivide and group

---

[1] Athanasius, *Or. in Arian.* i. 5.
[2] Philostorgius, ii. 15; cf. Hilarius, *de Trinitate*, xii. 34, etc.
[3] Socrates, v. 23. 1 and 3.

themselves around two of their bishops, Marinus himself and Agapius, whom Marinus had appointed as bishop of the Psathyrians in Ephesus. The two had not quarrelled on a point of doctrine: each of them simply claimed personal precedence over the other. Now, Agapius was supported in the fray by none other than Selenas, that Gothic bishop who had once been the secretary and had later become the successor of Ulfila himself (pp. 81, 116 above), and who was now presumably among his flock at Nicopolis. In the present series of disputes he had sided with the Psathyrians, holding that God had been the Father even when the Son did not yet exist. And his influence over the Goths at Constantinople was so vast that he was followed into Agapius' camp by nearly all of them. Indeed, the Goths gave such solid support to the Psathyrian party that when men wished to refer to the sect by a more serious name than 'Psathyrian' they called it simply the 'Goths'. So heated did tempers become over these disputes that a number of the Arian clergy became weary of the whole quarrel, abandoned their Arianism outright, and joined the Nicaeans. But the Goths, so far from tiring of it all, nearly took up arms against their opponents. Eventually, however, in 419 one of the Psathyrians named Plintha, a Goth who had become Master of Both Services and was regarded as the most powerful man in the Eastern Empire at the time, managed, not indeed to solve the original question which had caused the whole affair—that would certainly have been a noteworthy achievement—but to reconcile the factions in the capital, the basis of the reconciliation being that both sides should regard it as a law that the issue which had divided them should never be mentioned again. This agreement was confined to

Constantinople. Outside the capital the dispute was still in progress twenty years later when Socrates and Sozomen published their Histories, and we do not know how or when it finally ended.[1]

After the reconciliation in Constantinople the Goths made a gesture to their non-Psathyrian opponents by allotting a festival in their Church Calendar to the opposing leader Dorotheus, although he died a natural and not a martyr's death in 407 at the surprising age of 119.[2] Whatever may have been the ultimate reasons which caused the Goths to become involved in this theological dispute, there is no doubt that their emotions were stirred by it very deeply indeed; and it would seem from their behaviour during the affair that they had transferred to their bishop that whole-hearted loyalty with which in other days they had followed their elected chieftains.

3. Sunnia and Fretela

St. Jerome wrote a famous letter in reply to a communication from 'my most beloved brethren Sunnia and Fretela and the others who serve the Lord with you' (Ep. cvi). The date of this letter is an old puzzle: a not impossible guess is that it was written c. 405.[3] That the two Goths were Catholics and not Arians is shown by the affectionate terms in which Jerome addresses them, for he would not have wasted kindly words or his

---

[1] Socrates, v. 23; Sozomen, vii. 17. 9 ff.

[2] Gothic Calendar at 6 November; Delehaye, 277; R. Loewe, 'Der gotische Kalender', ZfdA, lix (1922), 245–90, at 271 ff.

[3] So J. Zeiller, Les origines chrétiennes dans les provinces danubiennes (Paris, 1918), 566, n. 3, and many others. There is a convenient translation of the letter into English in M. Metlen, 'Letter of St. Jerome to the Gothic Clergymen Sunnia and Frithila Concerning Places in their Copy of the Psalter which had been Corrupted from the Septuagint', Journal of English and Germanic Philology, xxxvi (1937), 515–42.

immense learning on a pair of barbarian heretics. They had written asking him to supply them with a comment on no fewer than 178 passages of the Psalms. What they wanted, according to Jerome (*Ep.* cvi. §2), was that he should indicate which reading best suited the Hebrew in cases where there was a divergency between the Greek text and the Latin of St. Jerome himself, which was based on the Hexapla edition of the Septuagint. The questions, in fact, turned upon the accuracy of the renderings of the Hebrew and the Greek in the Gallican Psalter which Jerome had completed in 392. In his reply Jerome raises no questions whatever regarding the text of Ulfila; nor does he make any reference at all, direct or indirect, to the existence of a Bible in Gothic, a language of which he knew nothing. There is no reason to suppose that the two Goths' questions were intended in the last resort to help them to test or to improve the Gothic text, and there is no evidence that they even knew of its existence:[1] they wanted nothing more than information on the conformity of the Gallican Psalter with the Greek and Hebrew. Perhaps Catholic Goths at this date would not care to concern themselves over-much with a text drawn up by so notorious an Arian as Ulfila.[2]

[1] *Contra*, G. W. S. Friedrichsen, *The Gothic Version of the Gospels* (Oxford, 1926), 197; Metlen, art. cit., 541 f.; but A. Wilmart, 'Les évangiles gothiques', *Revue biblique*, xxxvi (1927), 46–61, at 58 n. 3, rightly points out that it is a gratuitous assumption to hold that Sunnia and Fretela had an Ulfilan Psalter in front of them. Indeed, D. de Bruyne, 'La lettre de Jérome à Sunnia et Fretela sur le Psautier', *Zeitschrift für die neutestamentliche Wissenschaft*, xxviii (1929), 1–13, argues that Jerome's letter implies that they were comparing the Gallican Psalter, not with the Koinê, but with other Latin Psalters. But this is untenable: they had constantly referred to the Greek.

[2] The view that they were engaged on a critical edition of the Bible and that the Preface in the Codex Brixianus is their introduction to their work (so F. Kauffmann, 'Beiträge zur Quellenkritik der gotischen Bibelübersetzung', *Zeitschrift für deutsche Philologie*, xxxii (1900), 305–35,

139

Now, to have been able to understand the forty
printed pages of Jerome's reply as it stands in Labourt's
edition, swarming with niceties of exegesis and generously bespattered with Greek and Hebrew, these two
Goths must have spent years in the intensive study of
Greek and Latin and in acquiring an eye for textual
criticism. Yet such was their self-confidence that they
even dared to criticize the great and not always sweet-
tempered scholar, who does not hide his surprise at the
liberty which they had taken.[1] When they undertake
to tell him how he *ought* to have translated a phrase in
Psalm xlix, he tartly replies that 'it is clear even to fools'
that their translation cannot stand (§30 cf. §67).
Indeed, a more tactful saint might have refrained from
expressing at the beginning of his letter his astonishment
that such warlike hearts as those of the Goths should
seek after the *Hebraica veritas*, and might have omitted
to quote Acts, x. 34 'I perceive that God is no respecter
of persons'.

It is noteworthy that the scholarship of Sunnia and
Fretela was nothing if not meticulous; and some of the
questions which they asked concerned points of
extreme detail. In fact, at one point Jerome begs them
not to raise such tiny matters as make no difference
whatever to the sense of the text of the Psalms.[2] Thus,
in Psalm xliii they quote 'et non egredieris in virtutibus

esp. 316; J. Dräseke, 'Der Goten Sunja und Frithila Praefatio zum
Codex Brixianus', *Zeitschrift für wissenschaftliche Theologie*, i (1908),
107-17, is untenable: see Friedrichsen, op. cit., 196 ff.

[1] *Ep.* cvi. §30 'et miror quomodo vitium librarii dormitantis ad culpam
referatis interpretis', §54 'in Graeco invenisse vos dicitis "cui est auxilium
abs te", quod quia nos in Latina interpretatione vitamus, reprehendi-
mur', etc. Few scholars have been convinced by the ingenious argument
of de Bruyne, art. cit., that Sunnia and Fretela are fictitious and that
Jerome's letter was in fact designed for Romans.

[2] §54 'et quaeso vos ut huiusmodi ineptias et superfluas contentiones,
ubi nulla est sensus inmutatio, declinetis', *et al.*

nostris', and remark that in the Greek they read 'et non egredieris, Deus', etc. In Psalm lix they quote 'quis deducet me usque in Idumaeam?', and point out that the Greek has 'aut quis deducet me', etc. In Psalm xciii they quote 'beatus homo quem tu erudieris, Domine', and note that there is no 'tu' in the Greek. It has been assumed that men who paid attention to such minute matters of text, which could not possibly be relevant to doctrinal controversies, must have been drawing up a text of the Psalms for some editorial purpose, and there has been considerable controversy on what that purpose may have been. But this is untenable. Sunnia and Fretela are merely the spokesmen of their community, and Jerome's reply to their letter is addressed not to them alone but to the entire community: 'To my most beloved brethren Sunnia and Fretela and to the others who serve God along with you'. It will hardly be thought that the whole congregation was engaged on a communal translation or edition of the Psalms. It is safer to suppose that they wrote to the saint simply for the sake of their own religious education, and because of their pious desire for accurate knowledge, and because of their anxiety not to be incorrect in so holy a matter as the singing of the Psalms. Indeed, we are told explicitly that a problem in Psalm lxxiii was discussed very widely (§46). It is true that these men were far from free of that aridity which, as we have seen, characterized Germanic Arianism, but they were also educated in the Roman tradition: Cicero, Plautus, Terence, and Caecilius were more than names to them (§3), and Jerome has no qualms about quoting Virgil to them (§57) to establish his points.

It is noteworthy that the basis of their studies

(whatever the purpose of those studies may have been) was the Latin text of St. Jerome and not a Greek text, such as Ulfila had translated. It would not be true to say that they had no difficulties with the Latin language. Jerome is obliged to point out that one cannot say in Latin, 'adversus fratrem tuum detrahebas': it must be 'de fratre tuo detrahebas', and that the verb *amaricaverunt* does not exist (§§30, 67). But their difficulties with Greek are very much greater. Indeed, at one place their desire for a literal, word-for-word translation seems to have led them into a howler. Quoting Psalm xxviii 'et in templo eius omnis dicet gloriam', they mentioned, it seems, that the Greek is πᾶς τις. What their question was is not very clear, but it is ominous that Jerome has to point out that a literal translation of πᾶς τις by *omnis quis* would be absurd (§17). Moreover, at the end of their letter they had given a list of difficult Greek words which they asked the saint to translate into Latin for them; and the saint obliges at the end of *his* letter (§§86, cf. 63). All this suggests strongly that this was not a Gothic community living in Constantinople or elsewhere in the Eastern Empire, where Greek was the current language. Being more at home in Latin, they are more likely to have been living in the Latin-speaking part of the Empire. Of their community we can infer that it included, or that it was closely associated with, some Romans. A number of the questions raised by Sunnia and Fretela had also been raised more than once by a certain Avitus, who cannot be identified with certainty, but who was no doubt a Roman rather than a Greek (§§2, 86). Jerome's letter is addressed jointly to him and to Sunnia and Fretela and their community. Moreover, the original letter of the two Goths was delivered to Jerome by a priest called Firmus (§§2, 46);

and again it is unlikely that a man bearing this Latin name was a Greek. Now, in considering Psalm ci Sunnia and Fretela took the word δῶμα in its normal meaning of 'house'. But Jerome explains that in the Eastern provinces δῶμα has the same meaning as the word *tectum* bears 'with us': in Palestine and Egypt houses have flat roofs called δώματα, which in Rome are termed *solaria* or *Maeniana* (§63). Why does he explain the usage 'at Rome' specifically? Is it a fair inference that Sunnia and Fretela and their companions were living in the Western capital, where it would be not at all odd that they should associate with men bearing the Latin names Avitus and Firmus?

One or two comments may be made on the missionary work of St. John Chrysostom, on the Psathyrians, and on the studies of Sunnia and Fretela. These examples of the activities of Goths converted to Christianity after their arrival inside the Empire show what a long way the people had travelled since the days of the megistanes' persecution of the Christians in Gothia only a generation before. These men have moved not only into the economic and political relationships of the Roman Empire but also into the Roman thought-world. There may have been specifically Gothic elements in their thought, but the subject-matter of their thought is Roman. The questions which interested them were questions which had been thrown up by the development of Greco-Roman history, not by the development of native Gothic history. Although they retained their own language, their customs, and their Gothic social organization, they were clearly in process of being absorbed into Roman life. Moreover, the persons engaged in these activities were by no means the optimates alone, though it may have been from these that the initiative came.

The fervour with which the Goths of Constantinople threw themselves into the cause championed by Selenas could not have been inspired by the bishop alone: it was due to the men's own interest in questions of the nature of the Trinity. Such matters were as important to the Gothic soldiers of the East as they were to the inhabitants of Constantinople themselves.

But all this refers to those groups of Visigoths who had detached themselves from the great mass of their people and had remained behind in the Eastern capital when the bulk of the Visigoths had marched off to Italy and Gaul. Some, as we have guessed, may have taken up residence in Rome. We may wonder whether such men as Selenas and Sunnia and Fretela had as much in common with the warworn soldiers of Alaric far away in the West as they had with Roman priests like John Chrysostom and Marinus and Agapius and St. Jerome. The wonder is that the Visigoths retained their social identity for so long as in fact they did.

4. The Later History of Ulfila's Text

The Gothic Bible as now extant is the Bible which circulated among the Ostrogoths in Italy in the first half of the sixth century, and it must be used with caution as evidence for the character of the Bible as used among the Visigoths in Gaul in the fifth century. For it is known that very shortly after Ulfila had completed his work of translation Gothic scholars began to alter both his renderings and his readings in order to bring them into line with those of the Latin Bible—though not with Jerome's Vulgate—used by the populations through whose midst they passed. They were making a close study of the Latin versions of the Biblical text, as we know that Sunnia and Fretela were doing about the turn of the fourth and fifth centuries (though Sunnia and Fretela are not known to have concerned themselves with the Gothic text). But, ardent though their studies were, the Gothic scholars were not always judicious, and in at least a couple of places they altered the Gothic so as to make it render Latin readings which were themselves erroneous.[1] Moreover, this process of changing what Ulfila had written was not carried out systematically or with the same degree of intensity in all parts of the text of the Bible: it was done at random and in a haphazard way by a number of scholars over the years without (so far as we know) consultation or organization. A number of individual readers introduced changes into the text very much as the whim took them. There was no system about it, no official effort to produce a Revised Version of what Ulfila had written. Whatever Greek had been current among the Visigoths in the Danubian provinces was now extinct, and Greek scholarship was not flourishing in fifth-century Gaul, where they settled permanently in 418. Accordingly, even though Gothic scholars paid close attention to the Latin versions of the Bible which they found in the West or on their way to the West, their interest in the original Greek had died, and they were no longer in a position to occupy themselves with it.[2] In this they differed from their predecessors, Sunnia and Fretela, who consulted the Greek systematically, and from some

[1] In this section I am heavily indebted to the two splendid books of G. W. S. Friedrichsen, *The Gothic Version of the Gospels* (Oxford, 1926), and *The Gothic Version of the Epistles* (Oxford, 1939), to which I refer hereafter as *Gospels* and *Epistles* respectively. See *Epistles*, 210 *fin.*, 213, on 1 Timothy, vi. 10, 2 Timothy, iii. 4.
[2] Cf. Salvian, *de Gub. Dei*, v. 6 'nos [i.e. the Romans] ergo tantum scripturas sacras plenas inviolatas integras habemus, qui eas vel in fonte suo bibimus vel certe de purissimo fonte haustas per ministerium purae translationis haurimus'.

of their Ostrogothic successors of the early sixth century (p. 153 below).[1]

Latin influence on the Gothic text must have been accelerated when Gothic-Latin bilingual Bibles came into existence, as they must have done very soon after the general conversion of the people towards the end of the fourth century. They would have been required for administering oaths in the law-courts,[2] and for use in the army—this may have been the purpose for which the Gothic-Latin bilingual text was intended of which a fragment is preserved on a papyrus discovered somewhat west of Antinoe in Egypt[3]—or in congregations where some of the worshippers were Goths and others Romans (like the congregations to which Maximinus preached). At all events, fragments of two such Gothic-Latin bilinguals still exist, the Codex Carolinus at Wolffenbüttel and the Giessen papyrus. They show that textual influence was exerted in both directions: not only was the Gothic brought into line with the Latin, but the Latin also tended to be brought into line with the Gothic.[4] The Codex Brixianus contains a Latin

---

[1] The alterations of Ulfila's text are fully discussed by Friedrichsen, *Gospels*, 169 ff., *Epistles*, 180 ff.

[2] Cassiodorus, *Var.* iv. 12; Procopius, *BV* iv. 21. 21 (Vandals).

[3] It was assigned to the early fifth century by its first editors, P. Glaue and K. Helm, 'Das gotisch-lateinische Bibelfragment der Universitätsbibliothek zu Giessen', *Zeitschrift für die neutestamentliche Wissenschaft*, xi (1910), 1–38; but it is now generally agreed to date from the sixth century. W. Streitberg, *Die gotische Bibel*, ii (Heidelberg, 1910), who gives (pp. ix–xiv) the text of the papyrus and a brief discussion of its significance, suggests (p. xi) that the text may have been the possession of some Gothic military bishop or of some Gothic cleric who had been exiled to Antinoe. This last is the opinion of Glaue.

[4] This was first noticed by F. C. Burkitt, 'The Vulgate Gospels and the Codex Brixianus', *JTS*, i (1900), 129–34; cf. idem, 'A Gothic Latin Fragment from Antinoe', ibid., xi (1910), 611–13. His arguments have been worked out for Matthew and John by F. Kauffmann, 'Beiträge zur Quellenkritik der gotischen Bibelübersetzung: der Codex Brixianus', *Zeitschrift für deutsche Philologie*, xxxii (1900), 305–35, at 320 ff.

text which is in fact a copy of the Latin version of a
bilingual (if indeed it was not a Gothic-Latin-Greek
trilingual)[1] with the Gothic left out. Like the great
Codex Argenteus, which has preserved so much of
Ulfila's version of the Gospels, the Codex Brixianus is
written in silver ink on purple vellum, and both
manuscripts alike come from the one calligraphic
school of the earlier sixth century. The existence of
these bilingual texts invited the attentions of enthusiastic Gothic Biblical scholars and so caused the original
text of Ulfila to be further impaired.

Again, the studies of these Goths were also directed
to the Biblical commentaries produced by Latin
scholars, and in a number of passages they actually
replaced Ulfila's renderings by renderings and readings
derived from the Latin commentators, especially
Ambrosiaster. There can be little doubt that some
Gothic Christians immersed themselves in the study
of Western Catholic literature and were possibly
familiar with the works of the heretic Pelagius as well.[2]
Occasionally, indeed, even without the help of the
commentators, these scholars went so far as to alter the
Gothic in order to make it (as they thought) more
explicit, and in doing so they introduced ideas which
were not to be found in the Greek translated by Ulfila's
own Gothic. Nor were these changes always innocent or
well intentioned. It is a small matter that a bowdler has
spared Gothic sensibilities by omitting a reference to
homosexuality in 1 Timothy, i. 10.[3] But it would seem

---

[1] Kauffmann, art. cit., 319; cf. A. Wilmart, 'Les évangiles gothiques',
Revue biblique, xxxvi (1927), 46–61, at 56 f.; H. Lietzmann, 'Die Vorlage
der gotischen Bibel', *ZfdA*, lvi (1919), 249–78, at 265 (that the Brixianus
was a trilingual).
[2] Friedrichsen, *Epistles*, 214 ff.
[3] See E. Bernardt, *Vulfila* (Halle, 1875), xxx; Streitberg, ad loc.

that in one or two passages a distinct Arian bias can be traced in the mutilation of the Biblical text (p. 108, n. 3 above). This has been denied, to be sure, and we must not lightly believe, as used to be done, that Ulfila himself would have mistranslated deliberately in order to make the subordination of the Son to the Father quite explicit or in order to substitute *likeness* for *equality* in the description of the relationship between God the Father and God the Son at 1 Corinthians, xv. 25 ff., and Philippians, ii. 6, respectively.[1] If he had wished to make his points in this way, he might well have begun with John, x. 30, where in fact the text has not been tampered with. Moreover, paganism, as we have seen, by no means became extinct when the majority of the Visigoths were converted to Arianism, and in two or three passages of the Gothic Bible the rendering of the Greek has been distorted in order to make the text condemn pagan practices. For instance, it was no doubt some pagan practice that induced a Goth to alter Colossians, ii. 16, so as to include a reference to the full moon instead of to the new moon.[2] Elsewhere glosses have made their way into the text so as to remove the grounds for any offence that might be taken by readers of the original text: in Romans, ix. 13, for example, a gloss has been included in the text so as to eliminate the idea that God could so demean himself as to feel hatred.[3]

All these influences have been traced in the extant fragments of the Ostrogothic Bible, for behind those

---

[1] Friedrichsen, *Epistles*, 233, 236 ff.
[2] See Bernardt, op. cit., xxx. 527; Streitberg, ad loc.; Friedrichsen, *Epistles*, 152, 154 (on 1 Corinthians, x. 16), 183 (on Romans, xi. 16). It is interesting to see that the term νεομηνία is one of the words of which Sunnia and Fretela ask Jerome the precise meaning (*Ep.* cvi. 86).
[3] Streitberg, ad loc.; Friedrichsen, *Epistles*, 233.

silver words of the manuscripts there stand generations of writers and scholars and revisers of Ulfila's Gothic. But there is little reason to doubt that all these influences were already at work even in the reign of the first Visigothic king at Toulouse, Theodoric I (418–51). Indeed, we have explicit testimony to the damage which had already been done to the Gothic text by that time, and this evidence dates from less than a quarter of a century after the foundation of the kingdom of Toulouse. It consists of a capital passage of Salvian, a priest of Marseilles, who wrote his *De Gubernatione Dei* in 440 or 441. Salvian says that some barbarian peoples had a Biblical text which was interpolated and incorrectly handed down by the wicked authorities of earlier days; and if any among the barbarian nations have a text which is less interpolated and mutilated, their text is nonetheless 'corrupted by the tradition of teachers of old'. What such barbarians possess is an exegetical tradition rather than the unadulterated Scripture, and this tradition is an evil and tendentious one. The mass of the barbarians know nothing of Roman or any other scholarship and literature, and so they merely accept what their teachers say. They are familiar with the holy word not at first hand from their reading but at second hand from their teachers. The tradition of their teachers is like a law to them.[1]

From these statements of Salvian a number of conclusions can be drawn. In the first place, his reference is undoubtedly to the Visigoths and to a lesser extent to the Vandals, but not to the Ostrogoths.[2]

[1] Salvian, *de Gub. Dei*, v. 5 ff.
[2] From Salvian, v. 14, it is clear that his reference is to the Visigoths and Vandals alone, cf. vii. 38 'at non ita Gothi non ita Wandali, malis licet doctoribus instituti', etc. The only other Christian barbarians in Gaul in 440–1 were the Burgundians, and Salvian has not a single

149

At the time when he was writing in Gaul the bulk of the Ostrogoths were still enveloped in the darkness of the empire of Attila, and they were probably still pagan.[1] No doubt many individual Ostrogoths could be found in Constantinople throughout the first three quarters of the fifth century in the train of Plintha (p. 137 above), Ardaburius, and others. But the alien influences on the text of the Gothic Bible could not have been due to men living at Constantinople; for the distortions of the text were derived in some cases from the commentaries of Ambrosiaster and other Latin writers whose works are not likely to have been in the hands of Goths living in the Eastern capital. And influences derived from Eastern commentators, such as John Chrysostom, have not been clearly proved. In other words, when Latin commentators began to affect the text of Ulfila they affected the text which was carried about by the Visigoths of Alaric and his successors. Yet the fragments of the Bible in which modern scholars have traced them are an Ostrogothic production and were originally written in Ostrogothic Italy in the first half of the sixth century. It follows that the process of adapting Ulfila's text to the Latin was at some date taken over from the Visigoths by the Ostrogoths after they had settled in Italy in 489. The Latin element in the surviving fragments of Ulfila is not a peculiarly Ostrogothic phenomenon: it is the result of a process which had been begun by the Visigoths and was only later continued by the Ostrogoths. It does not follow that any specific corruption of Ulfila's text which can now

reference to them in any part of his work. On the use of the Bible among the Vandals see ibid., vii. 46.

[1] E. A. Thompson, 'Christianity and the Northern Barbarians', *apud* A. D. Momigliano (ed.), *Paganism and Christianity in the Fourth Century* (Oxford, 1963), 72–5.

be detected must have existed at one time in the Visigothic Bible used in Gaul in the fifth century: indeed, it may be that scarcely any of them did so. What Salvian's words show is that the *process* had been begun in his day, not that each individual corruption which made its way into the Visigothic text before 441 was necessarily taken over by the Ostrogoths. The principle of tampering with the text was a Visigothic, not an Ostrogothic, invention.

Secondly, in one respect of great importance Salvian's language suggests that there was a considerable difference between the text which he knew to exist among the Visigoths of his day and that which we know from the surviving fragments to have existed among the Ostrogoths in Italy. The terms which Salvian uses imply that the alterations which had crept into the Visigothic Bible were very extensive, and moreover that these wholesale alterations were distinctly tendentious.[1] It cannot have been very difficult in Salvian's day to point to passages in the text which had been altered so as to support the cause of Arianism. But that is not true of the Ostrogothic Bible of which we still possess fragments. In them no more than a couple of changes have been discovered after some generations of intensive study of the text; and even those which are commonly cited are by no means undisputed. It is not possible, in fact, to find a single undisputed example of a deliberate and tendentious Arian omission or excision from the text. Yet Salvian distinctly implies that such could be found not infrequently in the Visigothic text which circulated in the kingdom of Theodoric I. It looks as

[1] E. g. v. 6 'eadem, inquis, legunt illi quae leguntur a nobis. quomodo eadem, quae ab auctoribus quondam malis et male sunt interpolata et male tradita?' He refers to the barbarian text as *interpolata, vitiata, debilis, convulnerata, dilacerata, traditione corrupta.*

151

though the Ostrogoths, when they came once more in contact with the Visigoths, did not allow the worst features of Visigothic scholarship to find a place in their Bible. At any rate, the inference from Salvian's words would seem to be that among the Visigoths in the earliest days of their Gallic kingdom Arianism was more militant and more unscrupulous than it was to become in sixth-century Italy, where Goths and Romans lived side by side in considerable though not total amity.

Thirdly, Salvian's words imply that the mishandling of the Biblical text was nothing new in his day: he is quite clear that the practice had been going on for some considerable time before he wrote.[1] There is no reason to think that the process began only after the settlement at Toulouse in 418. It is more likely to have set in not many years after Ulfila died and may well have been under way during the period when Alaric was the leader of the main body of the Visigoths (395–410). It is greatly to be regretted that Jerome's letter to Sunnia and Fretela cannot be dated with any precision, for by the time when that letter was written some of the Visigoths appear to have already attained an impressive scholarly technique.

Finally, that the Arian clergy gave their Visigothic flock tendentious instruction in the Scriptures is obvious from Salvian's words, though whether their tendentiousness was greater than that of their Catholic counterparts it would not now be easy to say. But Salvian also makes it clear that Biblical scholarship was the possession of a small *élite* among the Visigoths to an extent that was not paralleled among the Catholic Roman population of Gaul. Moreover, this narrow

[1] Salvian, De Gub. Dei, v. 6 *quondam*, 7 *veterum*, 8 *doctrina inveterata*.

circle seems to have considered itself tightly bound by
the traditional interpretations of earlier scholars. They
were interested, Salvian implies, not in the Scriptural
truth, which could be elicited by study and thought,
but simply in the wicked, heretical tradition of their
own teachers. There was an absence of speculation and
originality, a hidebound traditionalism among Visigothic Arians which, as we have already seen, was a
characteristic of Germanic Arianism as a whole; and
criticism and argument and assistance were not forthcoming from the laity. Perhaps, indeed, the vast
majority of the rank and file of the Visigothic Arians
did not read the Bible because they could not read it:
they may have been still illiterate.

About the year 500 or a little later something of a
reaction took place among the Ostrogoths of Italy
against the loose treatment of the Biblical text which
had been common in Visigothic Gaul and which had
extended to the text of the Old Testament as well as to
that of the New.[1] We know something of this reaction
from the extant *Preface* bound in with the Brixian
bilingual Gothic-Latin Bible, of which the Latin version
alone survives. (The *Preface* is not in fact a preface to the
text contained in the Codex Brixianus as that text now
stands, but to the archetype of that text.)[2] The writer,
who was undoubtedly a well read scholar, begins with
an apt quotation from Rufinus' translation of the

[1] Streitberg, op. cit., xxxiv.
[2] For the text of the famous *Praefatio* see Kauffmann, art. cit., and (less
good) J. Dräseke, 'Der Goten Sunja und Frithila Praefatio zum Codex
Brixianus', *Zeitschrift für wissenschaftliche Theologie*, i (1908), 107–17, and
for a reprint of the text with an excellent commentary see Friedrichsen,
Gospels, 199–211, *Epistles*, 270 ff.; though refer also to M. Metlen, 'A
Natural Translation of the Praefatio Attached to the Codex Brixianus',
Journal of English and Germanic Philology, xxxvii (1938), 355–66; idem, 'The
Praefatio in the Codex Brixianus and Vulgar Latin'; ibid., xxxix (1940),
256–60.

153

Clementine *Recognitions* (viii. 37) on the need for exact translation of the Scriptures; and he proceeds to argue against an excessively literal, word-for-word translation and in favour of a fluent, idiomatic one. Evidently he was not altogether sympathetic to Ulfila's method of translating with extreme literalness, nor would he have been wholly favourable to Sunnia and Fretela if they had occupied themselves with the Gothic text, for Jerome's letter shows them to have been 'word sticklers who believe in the verbatim method of Bible translation at the expense not only of idiomatic usage but even of grammar'.[1] On the other hand, the author of the *Preface* protests against false and inaccurate renderings of an exegetical and misleading nature such as could be found, we may assume, among the Visigoths of the day. In defence of the readings which he has adopted the writer has worked out a system of annotations (*wultheres*, as he calls them) whereby the sign .gr. written over the annotation indicates that the note follows the Greek text literally, and the sign .la. indicates that it follows the Latin text literally.[2] It was not his intention, of course, to introduce new, conjectural readings of his own or to devise exegetical readings which would bring out what he believed to be the true sense of the passage in question. He undoubtedly confined himself to lections for which he had manuscript authority. The *Preface* illustrates the exact and detailed scholarship which the Goths had worked out for themselves when once they were lodged in the Roman world, and the thought which they had given to the technique of translation from Greek and Latin into Gothic. Whether

[1] Metlen, art. cit. ('A Natural Translation'), 541.
[2] On the *wultheres* see, in addition to the works cited in p. 153 n. 2 above, Burkitt, art. cit., 131 n. 1; Metlen, 'A Natural Translation', 363.

there was among the Visigoths any such movement as the author of the Brixian *Preface* recommends in favour of accurate but idiomatic renderings cannot now be said. It is all but certain, however, that they did not have at their disposal the Greek scholarship which the writer of the Brixian *Preface* had evidently mastered.

What is of the utmost importance for us in all this discussion of the Biblical scholarship of the Visigoths is the readiness and the thoroughness with which they had become Romanized. In spite of the difference of language and of sect which separated them from their Roman neighbours they had become deeply absorbed in the techniques of Roman scholarship and translation even in the reign of Theodoric I (418–51)and earlier.

5. Epilogue

When the armies of Justinian overthrew the Ostrogothic kingdom in 554, the Ostrogoths disappeared from the face of the earth. But, although Clovis drove the Visigoths from most of Gaul in 507, the Visigothic kingdom in Spain survived until the Muslims overran it in 711 and the following years. Throughout the entire period, from the times which we have been discussing until the beginning of the eighth century, the Visigoths never wholly fused with the Romans. At the Third Council of Toledo in 589 King Reccared and the Visigothic nobility announced their conversion to Catholicism; and henceforward Catholicism was the official religion of Spain. The tenets of the Council of Rimini, to which Ulfila had so fervently subscribed, were explicitly condemned and anathematized.[1] All Arian books that could be found were surrendered to the King: they were placed in one house, which was

[1] III Toledo 27 (Mansi, ix. 986).

155

then set on fire, and all were destroyed.[1] The result was that not a single Gothic text has survived in Spain. When the Gothic language ceased to be spoken we do not know: our sources for the history of Visigothic Spain are silent on the fate of the language in which Ulfila wrote. In the seventh century the old Gothic style of dress had disappeared, the custom of burying goods along with the dead had been abandoned, and Gothic art-styles were replaced by East Roman ones. Yet the Visigoths retained their identity to the end and always felt themselves to be different from the Romans in whose midst they had lived for so many generations. The process of absorption, which was going on so rapidly in the fifth century, was never brought to completion.

[1] Fredegarius, iv. 8 (p. 7, ed. J. M. Wallace-Hadrill).

WAS FRITIGERN A CHRISTIAN?

FRITIGERN, who led the Visigothic army when they inflicted their overwhelming defeat on the Emperor Valens at Adrianople, is generally believed to have been a Christian. But if we reject as apocryphal the story of his war against Athanaric, what evidence remains? Nothing except an astonishing conjectural reading which has been almost universally admitted into the surviving fragment of the Gothic Calendar. This is the conjecture *Frithagairnis* for *Frithaireikeis* (or rather *Frithaireikeikeis*, an obvious slip) of the manuscript. Against this it may be urged (i) that it is quite arbitrary and suggests that because we do not happen to hear of Frederic elsewhere, he never existed; (ii) that the change is palaeographically improbable; and (iii) that the conjecture makes Fritigern not only a Christian but even a martyr! Yet it has rarely been rejected since it was proposed by W. Krafft in 1854. As for the fact that Fritigern used a Christian priest as intermediary in his negotiations with Valens in 378, this throws no light on his personal beliefs. Who would consider that the chief who sent Ulfila to Constantinople in 341 as ambassador was himself a Christian, or that Theodoric I of Toulouse was a Catholic because he negotiated with Litorius and Aetius through Catholic bishops? These envoys were no doubt used because those who sent them believed that they would have more influence on the Roman authorities than heretic or pagan barbarians were likely to have. Until new arguments are put forward, it would be well to consider that Fritigern was a pagan like the great bulk of the warriors whom he led at Adrianople.

At all events, there is not the slightest reason for thinking that Fritigern and Ulfila cooperated with each other at any time in their lives.

GAATHA

ALL that we know of Gaatha is derived from the
account of the twenty-six martyrs.[1] The chief who
burned the church over their heads was called Winguric. Their remains were gathered up by Gaatha,
the queen of the nation of the Goths, who was a
Christian and orthodox—orthodox, that is, according
to the views of the author. Leaving her realm to her son
Arimerius, she travelled to the Roman Empire in the
company of her daughter Dulcilla. She then sent a
message to Arimerius, went to join him, and returned
with him. She left Dulcilla in Cyzicus. Wella, who had
helped her to collect the remains of the martyrs, went
back to Gothia along with Gaatha and was stoned to
death. At a later date Dulcilla died peacefully.

This is a scarcely coherent fragment of a narrative;
but it contains one or two matters of interest. Gaatha is
described as 'the wife of the other leader of the nation
of the Goths', a phrase which distinctly implies the
existence of the dual leadership which is attested
elsewhere for the Visigoths and numerous other
Germanic peoples.[2] This kind of joint rule is found only
in the confederate leadership and does not occur in the
case of the leadership of the *pagi* or of any other unit
than that of the people as a whole. It follows that the
confederation of the tribes (p. 43 f. above) was in
existence at this time (383–92). There is no evidence

---

[1] See the Synaxary printed by Achelis, art. cit. (on p. 84 n. 3 above)
318 f.
[2] See Thompson, *EG*, 39.

whatever for the view that Gaatha was the widow of Fritigern.

There is a difficulty in the words which describe her journey to the Roman Empire: τόπον ἐκ τόπου ἀμείβουσα ἦλθεν ἕως τῆς γῆς τῶν ᾿Ρωμαίων. This implies that the country from which she set out was not 'Roman territory'. Now, it cannot be argued that Gaatha was an Ostrogoth and that the reference is to some place in southern Russia: that would not be consistent with Sozomen, vi. 37. 13 f., who unquestionably refers to the same incident and the same community.[1] I take it that Gaatha lived in Moesia, and that our very abbreviated authority has used a phrase of which one implication— that Moesia was not now Roman but Visigothic—is inaccurate. Even when the Visigoths lived as Federates in Moesia, Moesia did not cease to be a Roman province.

The view that Wella was lynched by infuriated Arians because he had apostatized to the semi-Arians,[2] is scarcely likely to be accepted. For a Gepid named Οὐέλας see Procopius, BG vii. 1. 43, and for a Sueve called Vella see J. Vives, Inscripciones cristianas de la España romana y visigoda (Barcelona, 1942), no. 504.

[1] Delehaye, 280 f.
[2] Proposed by Loewe, art. cit. (on p. 138 n. 2 above), 266.

THE BISHOP GODDA

LITTLE attention has been paid by scholars to the bishop Godda,[1] who is known only from the *Passio SS. Innae, Rimae, et Pinnae* printed in Delehaye, 215 f. From this we learn that during a certain winter the three saints were put to death by drowning after they had converted many barbarians. Seven years after their martyrdom Bishop Godda gathered their remains, carried them on his own back to an unnamed place in Gothia, and buried them there. Later (καὶ μετὰ ταῦτα) he took them to the harbour Haliscus, a place which has never been identified (p. 29 above). According to the author of the *Passio*, the date of the martyrdom was unknown. Hence the Church celebrated the date of the final burial of the bones.

This narrative raises two important questions, and I confess that I cannot answer either of them satisfactorily: (i) In what year did the martyrdom take place? and (ii) To which sect did the bishop Godda belong? Only two persecutions of the Christians in Gothia are reported from the fourth century, that of 347–8, which resulted in Ulfila's flight from Gothia, and that of 369–72, in which Saba met his death. Let us consider the later persecution first. Peace between Valens and the Visigoths was arranged in the summer of 369,[2] and immediately after it the persecution began. The guess that Inna and his companions were martyred at the

---

[1] With his name compare that of the Goth Γώδας in Procopius, *BV* iii. 10. 25.
[2] Themistius, *Or.* x. 134 A.

beginning of the persecution, i.e. in the winter of 369–70, comes up against difficulties which by no means disappear if we suppose that the winter mentioned in the *Passio* is that of 370–1 or that of 371–2. For if they died in 369–70, we must believe that Godda collected their bodies late in 376 and brought them to Haliscus later still. But the Huns had occupied Gothia in the summer of 376, and in the autumn of that year the Visigoths had crossed the Danube. Is it conceivable that Godda was able to travel freely and without interference in Gothia under the ferocious rule of the Huns and after his fellow-countrymen had fled to the Roman Empire? Is it not likely that our source, abbreviated though it is, would have given some hint of the dangers which would have threatened him at the hands of the nomads? The experiences of Theotimus, bishop of Tomi, who tried to travel in Hun territory at precisely this time,[1] suggest that this omission is unlikely; and nothing is gained if we date the martyrdom one or two years later and place the travels of Godda in 377 or 378. Moreover, if Godda was in a position to carry off the bodies after the Huns had occupied Gothia, we should have expected him to have taken them to the Roman provinces rather than to have left them in a country which practically all Christians had abandoned. Even before the arrival of the Huns it had been thought fitting to take the bodies of Nicetas (if he ever existed) and Saba to Asia Minor.

None of these considerations brings us to a definite result; but, particularly in view of the adventures of Theotimus, our safest course would seem to be to suppose that Inna, Rema, and Pinna were martyred in the winter of 347–8 and that Godda transferred their

[1] Sozomen, vii. 26. 6 ff.

bodies in 354. At that date he could have travelled in Gothia without interference or danger.

Was Godda a Catholic? There is no evidence, and in my opinion it is unlikely, that there was a second Arian bishop in Gothia in the days of Ulfila. Our sources continually refer to Ulfila as 'the bishop of the Goths' or 'the bishop of the people'.[1] Similarly, his secretary and successor, Selenas, is referred to only as 'the bishop of the Goths';[2] and it is noteworthy that, although Selenas presumably continued to live in the settlement at Nicopolis, he was able to influence profoundly the Gothic troops at Constantinople (p. 137 above). There is no evidence that in his time there was one Visigothic bishop at Nicopolis and another at Constantinople. Even in the fifth century the bulk of the Visigoths, i.e. those who followed Alaric to the West, appear to have had only one bishop. This was Sigesarius, who like his predecessors Ulfila and Selenas, is termed 'the bishop of the Goths', not 'a Gothic bishop' or 'one of the Gothic bishops' or the like.[3] But H. von Schubert, *Staat und Kirche in den arianischen Königreichen* (1912), 64 ff., thinks that Sigesarius was probably a 'Patriarch' who stood at the head of the Visigothic bishops as the Vandal Patriarch headed the Arian Vandal bishops after the foundation of the Vandal kingdom in Africa. But it is not clear that we are justified in drawing inferences from conditions in the barbarian kingdoms, with their old established cities, to those of the Migrations, when the various peoples were continually on the move; and if von Schubert is right, it is curious that our sources

[1] Socrates, ii. 41. 23, iv. 33. 6; Sozomen, iv. 24. 1, vi. 37. 6, vii. 17. 12; Philostorgius, ii. 5 (p. 17. 18), where, as Bidez proposes, we ought undoubtedly to read ἐπίσκοπος.
[2] Socrates, v. 23. 8; Sozomen, vii. 17. 11.
[3] Sozomen, ix. 9. 1; Olympiodorus of Thebes, frag. 26.

never mention or even imply the existence of the suffragan bishops. So we have no valid ground for believing that there was a plurality of Visigothic bishops before the foundation of the kingdom of Toulouse in 418. Hence, it would seem to follow that Godda, Inna, Rema, and Pinna were Catholics.

It is not clear whether Godda was the first Catholic bishop of the Visigoths, since it has not yet been decided whether Theophilus, bishop of 'Gothia',[1] who attended the Council of Nicaea in 325, was a Visigoth from north of the lower Danube or an Ostrogoth from the Crimea. The name *Gothia* was used of the Crimean settlements as well as of the Danubian settlements;[2] and I have not been convinced that Theophilus was a Visigoth. We can only conclude that, if Theophilus was a Visigoth, Godda was not the first Catholic bishop to minister to the Visigoths; but if Theophilus was an Ostrogoth, then Godda *was* the first Visigothic Catholic bishop—he was perhaps appointed so as to counter the success which Ulfila was winning for Arianism among the barbarians after 341. However that may be, we know of no other Catholic Visigothic bishop before the reign of King Leovigild (568–86).

If these hypotheses are acceptable—and I do not see how we can go beyond hypotheses—it would follow that Catholics as well as Arians were persecuted in 347–8, as was certainly the case in 369–72. There is evidence in Cyril of Jerusalem[3] for the presence of Catholics among the Goths during the first persecution. It would also follow that these Catholics were numerous enough to justify the appointment of a bishop to guide

<hr />

[1] On the forms of the name in the manuscripts see A. A. Vasiliev, *The Goths in the Crimea* (Cambridge, Mass., 1936), 12.

[2] John Chrysostom, *Epp.* xiv, ccvi.

[3] *Catech.* x. 19 (Migne, *PG* xxxiii. 687).

them. But the later fortunes of the bishopric, like so much that has to do with Visigothic Catholicism, are wholly unknown. The only Catholic Gothic bishop of a later date (before the reign of Leovigild) whose existence is attested is the Ostrogoth Unila, to whom John Chrysostom refers in one of his letters (*Ep.* xiv). But Godda was not an Ostrogoth, for, so far as we know, the Ostrogothic chieftains in the Crimea never persecuted the Christians who lived among them.

APPENDIX FOUR
THE *PASSION OF ST. SABA THE GOTH*

John Matthews, Yale University

Introduction

The trials and execution of the Gothic martyr Saba are narrated in the form of a letter from the Christian church in Gothia to its fellow-churches in Cappadocia and elsewhere. Though set in Gothic territory and describing an event there, the text is composed within an established tradition of Greek martyrology. It begins and ends with an evocation of the second-century *Passion of Polycarp* (nn. 2 and 24 below); while the narrative of the martyrdom of Saba is followed by an account of the recovery of his relics by Junius Soranus, *dux Scythiae*[1] and by an exhortation to the churches in the Roman empire to celebrate the day of martyrdom, which is given as 12 April in the consular year 372. The text contains numerous reminiscences of the Greek New Testament, notably in its introductory sentences, in passages of reported or direct speech, and at points where the author of the *Passion* is attributing motive and sentiment to its central character. The literary and liturgical, as well as historical dimensions of the *Passion* should be borne in mind by anyone approaching the text as a historical document about Gothic society. Nevertheless, the picture of the village community that it presents fits well the

---

[1] A.H.M. Jones, J.R. Martindale, J. Morris, *Prosopography of the Later Roman Empire*, I (1971), p. 848 (Soranus 2). Also addressed to Soranus is Basil, *Ep.* 165 (of 374).

character of the Sîntana (or Sântana) de Mures archaeological culture briefly described by Thompson in Chapter 2 of his book (pp. 34ff.), and in comprehensive detail (as of the date of publication) by Peter Heather in Chapter 3 of Heather and Matthews, *The Goths in the Fourth Century* (Liverpool University Press, 1991). In considering the historicity of the *Passion*, it is also worth noting that the date attributed to the martyrdom is internally consistent; in the year 372, 12 April did fall on a Thursday.

To judge by the reference to the church of Cappadocia, and the part played in the recovery of the relics by Junius Soranus, the ecclesiastical dignitary addressed in the last paragraph of the text was Basil of Caesarea, whose connections with Soranus in this matter are attested in his *Letter* 155, which is addressed to him and mentions people 'setting out for Scythia'. As with other texts of this nature, an important part of the function of the *Passion* is to authenticate the circumstances of martyrdom in order to validate the cult founded upon it. The Roman province of Scythia, from which the recovery of the relics was initiated, was in easy communication with the Gothic territories beyond the Danube. It may be that the text of the *Passion*, and the relics of the martyred saint, were transmitted to Roman Asia Minor by a senior cleric in Scythia, such as Betranion bishop of Tomi (modern Constanta).

The text survives in two manuscripts, in the libraries of St. Mark's at Venice (tenth-eleventh century) and the Vatican (early tenth century). The first publication, from the Vatican manuscript, was in *Acta Sanctorum*, April, II, pp. 966-8 (published 1675), and the first critical edition by H. Delehaye, *Analecta Bollandiana* 31 (1912), 216-21; hence the most generally accessible text in Knopf-

THE *PASSION OF ST. SABA THE GOTH*

Krüger, *Ausgewählte Märtyrerakten* (4th ed. by G. Ruhbach, 1965), 119-24.

Translation

The church of God dwelling in Gothia, to the church of God dwelling in Cappadocia and all the other communities of the holy catholic church in any place; may the mercy, peace and love of God the Father and our Lord Jesus Christ be multiplied.[2]

I.1. Now more than ever is the saying of the blessed Peter proved true, that 'in every nation he that feareth God and worketh righteousness is acceptable to him' [*Acts* 10.35]. This is confirmed now in the story of the blessed Saba, who is a witness of God and our Saviour Jesus Christ. **2.** For this man, a Goth by race[3] and living in Gothia, shone out like a light in the firmament, 'in the midst of a crooked and perverse generation' [*Phil.* 2.15], imitating the saints and eminent in their company in upright actions according to Christ. **3.** For from childhood he sought after nothing else but piety to our Saviour and Lord Jesus Christ, thinking this to be perfect virtue, to attain perfect manhood in knowledge of the Son of God [cf. *Eph.* 4.13]. **4.** And since 'to them that love God all things work together for good' [*Rom.* 8.28], he attained 'the prize of the high calling' [*Phil.* 3.14], which he had desired from his youth; then, striving face

---

[2] The first and last paragraphs of the *Passion* imitate the corresponding sections of the *Passion of Polycarp*; cf. H. Musurillo, *Acts of the Christian Martyrs* (1972), 2f., 16ff.

[3] It is interesting that this point should be made explicitly, given the fact that many Gothic Christians (such as Ulfila) were descended from Roman prisoners taken from Asia Minor by its third-century invaders; indeed, the name of Saba(s) himself seems more Syrian or Cappadocian than Gothic (though see Thompson 84, n. 3). There may through intermarriage have been many of mixed descent who counted as full members of Gothic society.

to face against the enemy and overcoming the evils of this life and always being peaceable to all, for the sake of his memory and the edification of the worshippers of God after his liberation in the Lord, he bade us not be idle but write of his triumphs.

II.1. Now Saba was orthodox in faith,[4] devout, prepared for every sort of just obedience, a kindly man, 'rude in speech yet not in knowledge' [*II Cor.* 11.6], speaking peaceably to all on behalf of truth, reproaching the idolaters and not 'exalted overmuch' [cf. *II Cor.* 12.7], but 'condescending to men of low estate' [*Rom.* 12.16] as is fitting, tranquil, not impetuous in speech, most zealous for every good work [cf. *Titus* 1.16]. **2.** He sang God's praise in church and this was his special concern.[5] He took thought neither for money nor for possessions except the bare necessities. He was temperate, self-controlled in all things, uninitiated in woman, abstinent, observed all fasts, was steadfast in prayers without vainglory and subjected all men to his good example. He performed the work required of him and was no busybody in what did not concern him [cf. *II Thess.* 3.11]. In sum he preserved an unblemished 'faith working through love' [*Gal.* 5.6], never hesitating to speak out on all occasions in the Lord.

III.1. Not once but many times before his consummation did he display a pious deed in faith. On

---

[4] This claim of orthodoxy is no doubt designed to counter the association of Gothic orthodoxy with the Arian beliefs of Ulfila, not to mention the emperor Valens.

[5] The Greek words, *psallôn en ekklesiâ*, might be a purely general reference to worship in church, but the comment that this was Saba's 'special concern' implies something more specific, such as that he was *lector*, or possibly *cantor*, of his local church; we might expect the persecution to focus on the presbyter and lesser clergy. Ulfila too was *lector* before his consecration as bishop; see the *Letter* of Auxentius translated in Heather and Matthews, *The Goths in the Fourth Century*, 145-53, at 150.

the first occasion when the chief men[6] in Gothia began to be moved against the Christians, compelling them to eat sacrificial meat, it occurred to some of the pagans in the village in which Saba lived to make the Christians who belonged to them eat publicly before the persecutors meat that had not been sacrificed in place of that which had, hoping thereby to preserve the innocence of their own people and at the same time to deceive the persecutors. **2.** Learning this, the blessed Saba not only himself refused to touch the forbidden meat but advanced into the midst of the gathering[7] and bore witness, saying to everyone, 'If anyone eats of that meat, this man cannot be a Christian', and he prevented them all from falling into the Devil's snare. For this, the men who had devised the deception threw him out of the village, but after some time allowed him to return. **3.** On another occasion when a time of trial was moved in customary fashion by the Goths, some of the pagans from the same village intended while offering sacrifices to the gods to swear to the persecutor

---

[6] The Greek word *megistânes*, referred by Thompson (64ff.) to the Gothic *optimates* or tribal nobility, is a more general word in Biblical Greek, used for instance of the 'lords' of Herod the Great at *Mark* 6.21, and is not to be identified or connected with any particular Gothic position or status. The phase of persecution envisaged at this point is clearly distinct from the 'great persecution' of IV.1ff., but it is not clear by how much it precedes it, or how the two phases are connected. Z. Rubin saw a reference back to events of 347/8 (*Mus. Helv.* 38 [1981], at 44), but it is unlikely that the text would jump 25 years between III.5 and IV.1; further, according to VII.5 Saba was 38 years old in 372, and so would have been only 13 or 14 in 347/8.

[7] The nature of the gathering is not defined (at III.4 a village council, or *sunedrion*, is mentioned). It is suggested by Thompson (68f.), that the eating of the meat is intended to represent a communal meal symbolising the social unity of the village, but it can more simply be seen as a straightforward traditional test of belief. As on the earlier occasion (II.1-2) the Gothic community seems more anxious to protect its members from harm than to preserve religious solidarity.

170

that there was not a single Christian in their village. **4.** But Saba, again speaking out, came forward in the midst of their council and said, 'Let no man swear on my account, for I am a Christian'. Then in the presence of the persecutor, the villagers who were hiding away their friends swore that there was no Christian in the village, except one. **5.** Hearing this, the leader of the outrage ordered Sabas to stand before him. When he stood there, the persecutor asked those who brought him forward whether he had anything among his possessions. When they replied, 'Nothing except the clothes he wears', the lawless one set him at nought and said, 'Such a man can neither help nor harm us',[8] and with these words ordered him to be thrown outside.

IV.1 Afterwards, when a great persecution was stirred by the infidels in Gothia against the church of God, as the holy day of Easter approached,[9] Saba resolved to go away to another village[10] to the presbyter Gouththikâs to celebrate the feast with him. As he was walking along the road, the figure of a huge man, radiant in form, appeared and said to him: 'Turn around and return to Sansalâs the presbyter'. Saba replied to the figure, 'Sansalâs is away from home'. **2.** In fact Sansalâs was in flight because of the persecution and was spending time

---

[8] No doubt Saba's lack of possessions has something to do with his position in the church (above, n. 5); perhaps he should be seen as a sort of Gothic monk, like the 'humiles' found in the company of a presbyter at Ammianus Marcellinus 31.12.8. The identity of the 'leader of the outrage' mentioned in this passage is not known; presumably a member of the tribal authorities external to the village.

[9] For the date, cf. below, nn. 14, 16-17, 22.

[10] The Greek word is *polis*, a city, but this would be a misleading translation (cf. Thompson 6, n. 3). What is meant is a village community such as was characteristic of Gothic settlement.

171

in Romania,[11] but at that time had just come back to his home on account of the holy day of Easter. Saba did not know anything about his return, and that is why he replied in this fashion to the figure that appeared to him, and strove to continue his journey to Gouththikâs the presbyter. **3.** While he was refusing to obey the instruction given him, suddenly, although the weather was fine at that time,[12] a huge fall of snow appeared on the face of the earth, so that the road was blocked and it was impossible to pass. **4.** Then Saba realised that it was the will of God that prevented him from proceeding further and told him to return to the presbyter Sansalâs; and praising the Lord he turned and went back. When he saw Sansalâs he rejoiced and told him and many others[13] of the vision he had seen on the road. **5.** So they celebrated together the festival of Easter. Then, on the third night after the festival,[14] there came at the behest of the impious ones Atharidus, the son of Rothesteus of royal rank, with a gang of lawless bandits.[15] He fell on the

[11] It is interesting that Sansalâs finds refuge from persecution in the Roman empire, presumably with a Christian community there: one thinks of the church at Durostorum (Silistra) on the Danube, or the Gothic Christian settlement established by Ulfila at Nicopolis in Moesia, mentioned much later by Jordanes (*Getica* 267). Such a community might have been instrumental in transmitting the known facts about the martyrdom of Saba to the author of the *Passion*.

[12] Perhaps, if anything so specific is meant, 'at that time (of day)' rather than 'at that season (of the year)'; but the latter is an attractive reading – an unexpected springtime snowfall in hitherto fine weather.

[13] This phrase, like the incidents of the oath (III.4) and the sacrificial meat (III.1), suggests that there was a considerable number of Christians in the village. For a suggestion as to how Sansalâs and Saba were chosen for punishment, see n. 5.

[14] The 'third night after the festival' takes us from Easter Sunday to Tuesday night.

[15] Rothesteus and Atharidus are otherwise unknown. The 'gang of lawless bandits' looks like a reference to the *comitatus* (retinue or following) of a Germanic leader, an institution mentioned also, for the Goths, by Ammianus

village, where he found the presbyter asleep in his house
and had him tied up. Saba also he seized naked from his
couch and likewise threw into bonds. **6.** The presbyter
they held captive on a wagon, but they took Saba naked
as he was and drove him throughout the thickets which
they had just burned, following closely behind and
beating him with rods and scourges, carried away by
pitiless cruelty against the servants of God.

V.1. Yet the harshness of his enemies confirmed the
patience and faith of the just man. When day came,[16]
Saba, glorying in the Lord, said to those who had
persecuted him, 'Did you not drive and beat me across
burned wastes, onto the sharp points of thorns, naked
and without shoes? See, whether my feet are injured and
whether I have weals on my body from this, or from the
beatings you inflicted upon me'. **2.** When they looked
and no trace was seen on his flesh of the pitiless things
they had done, they lifted up the axle of a wagon and put
it on his shoulders, and stretched out his hands and tied
them to the ends of the axle. In the same way they also
stretched out his feet and tied them to another axle.
Finally they threw him down on the axles and let him lie
on his back upon the ground, and until far into the night
went on flogging him without respite. **3.** When the
torturers had fallen asleep, a woman came up and set him
free; she was a woman working at night to prepare food
for the people in the house.[17] Set free, Saba remained in
the same place without fear, and joined the woman at her

(31.5.6); cf. Thompson, 51ff. A classic discussion, translated into English, is W.
Schlesinger, 'Lord and followers in German institutional history', in F.C.
Cheyette (ed.), *Lordship and Community in Medieval Europe* (New York, 1968), 64-99.

[16] Viz. Wednesday morning.

[17] The night of Wednesday/Thursday. The woman must be the slave or
servant of a leading household of the village.

work. When day came,[18] the impious Atharidus ordered Saba to have his hands bound and to be suspended from the beam of the house.

VI.1 A little later came the men sent by Atharidus, bringing sacrificial meat, and they said to the presbyter and to Saba, 'Atharidus ordered these things to be brought to you, that you may eat and save your souls from death'. **2.** The presbyter replied and said, 'We shall not eat these things, for it is not possible for us to do so. Now, tell Atharidus to order us to be crucified, or put to death by whatever method he may choose'. **3.** Saba said, 'Who is it that gave these orders?' They replied, 'Our lord Atharidus'. And Saba said, 'There is one Lord, God in heaven; but Atharidus is a man, impious and accursed. And this food of perdition is impure and profane, like Atharidus who sent it'. **4.** When Saba said this, one of the attendants of Atharidus in a blazing fit of anger seized a pestle and hurled it like a javelin hard against the breast of the saint, so that the onlookers thought that Saba would be shattered by the violence of the blow and die on the spot.[19] **5.** But Saba, his longing for piety overcoming the pain of the inflictions laid upon him, said to the executioner, 'Now, you suppose that you have struck me with the pestle: but let me tell you this, that so far am I feeling pain, that I would suppose you had hurled at me a skein of wool'. **6.** And he provided a clear proof of the truth of his words, for he neither cried out nor groaned as if in pain nor was there any trace whatever of the blow to be seen on his body.

---

[18] Sc. of Thursday, the day of Saba's final inquisition and execution.

[19] Ammianus describes how some Goths fought in battle by hurling fire-hardened clubs (31.7.13). The pestle, hurled by a practised arm, would form a somewhat similar (if much smaller) implement.

VII.1. Finally Atharidus, learning all this, ordered him to be put to death. Those appointed to perform this lawless act left the presbyter Sansalâs in bonds, and took hold of Saba and led him away to drown him in the river called the Mousaios.[20] **2.** But the blessed Saba, remembering the injunction of the Lord and loving his neighbour as himself [*Mark* 12.33, etc.], said, 'What has the presbyter done wrong, that he does not die with me?' They replied to him, 'This is no concern of yours'. **3.** When they said this, Saba burst out in exultation of the Holy Spirit and said, 'Blessed are you, Lord, and glorified is your name, Jesus, for ever and ever, amen [cf. Septuagint *Daniel* 3.52, 56]: for Atharidus has pierced himself through with eternal death and destruction, and sends me to the life that remains for ever; so well pleased are you in your servants, O Lord our God'. **4.** And along the entire road he uttered thanks to God as he was led along, thinking 'the sufferings of the present time not worthy to be compared with the glory which would be revealed to the saints' [*Rom.* 8.18]. When they came to the banks of the river, his guards said to one another, 'Come now, let us set free this fool. How will Atharidus ever find out?' But the blessed Saba said to them, 'Why do you waste time talking nonsense and not do what you were told to? For I see what you cannot see: over there on the other side, standing in glory, the saints who have come to receive me'. **5.** Then they took him down to the water, still thanking and glorifying God (until the very end his soul performed worship), threw him in and, pressing a beam against his neck, pushed him to the bottom and held him there. So made perfect through

---

[20] For the river Mousaios as the Buzau see Thompson, 66.

wood and water,[21] he kept undefiled the symbol of salvation, being thirty-eight years of age. **6.** His consummation took place on the fifth day of the Sabbath after Easter, which is the day before the Ides of April, in the reign of Valentinian and Valens the Augusti, and in the consulship of Modestus and Arintheus (12 April 372).[22]

VIII.1. Then his executioners pulled him out of the water and went away leaving him unburied; but neither dog nor any wild beast at all touched his body, but it was gathered up by the hand of the brethren and his remains laid to rest. These Junius Soranus, *vir clarissimus*, *dux* of Scythia, one who honoured the Lord, sending trustworthy men transported from barbarian land to Romania.[23] **2.** And favouring his own native land with a precious gift and a glorious fruit of faith, he sent the remains to Cappadocia and to your Piety, carrying out the wishes of the college of presbyters, the Lord ordaining matters to please the brethren who obey and fear him. **3.** Therefore, celebrating spiritual communion on the day in which he fought for and carried off the

[21] Basil of Caesarea, *Letter* 164, to ?Betranion of Tomi, refers to martyrdoms by 'wood and water'. Execution by drowning under wooden frames is mentioned by Tacitus (*Germania* 12.1), and the practice is attested by archaeological discoveries of human remains preserved in bogs and marshes, with systematically inflicted fatal wounds. In this case, the executioners retrieved the body and left it exposed.

[22] The transmitted text, presumably by incorporation of a confused marginal annotation, reads at this point 'in the [consulship of Flavius] Valentinianus and Valens. [These are found] in the consulship of Modestus and Arintheus'. The translation incorporates the necessary corrections, by the respective amendment and deletion of the phrases shown in square brackets. Easter Thursday in 372 did in fact fall on 12 April (Delehaye, 291).

[23] This 'recovery party' is no doubt that mentioned by Basil in his letter to Junius Soranus (see above). The 'college of presbyters' mentioned at VIII.2 was presumably that of a church in Scythia, possibly Tomi; 'your Piety' (*theosebeia*) in VIII.2 is Basil of Caesarea.

crown, tell also the brethren in those parts, in order that they may perform joyful celebrations in every holy and catholic church, praising the Lord who chooses the elect from among his own servants. **4.** Salute all the saints; those who, with you, are being persecuted, salute you. To him who can gather all of us by his grace and bounty into his kingdom in heaven be glory, honour, power and majesty, with his only-begotten Son and Holy Spirit for ever and ever, Amen.[24]

---

[24] For the closing allusions to the *Passion of Polycarp* (20.1; 22.3), see above, n. 2.

INDEX

www.ingramcontent.com/pod-product-compliance
Ingram Content Group UK Ltd.
Pitfield, Milton Keynes, MK11 3LW, UK
UKHW020716280225
455688UK00012B/392